GENOCIDE **&** PERSECUTION

| Darfur

Titles in the Genocide and Persecution Series

GENOCIDE & PERSECUTION

I Darfur

Noah Berlatsky
Book Editor

Frank Chalk
Consulting Editor

GREENHAVEN PRESS
A part of Gale, Cengage Learning

DISCARDED

GALE
CENGAGE Learning·

Farmington Hills, Mich • San Francisco • New York • Waterville, Maine
Meriden, Conn • Mason, Ohio • Chicago

Patricia Coryell, *Vice President & Publisher, New Products & GVRL*
Douglas Dentino, *Manager, New Products*
Judy Galens, *Acquisitions Editor*

For more information, contact:
Greenhaven Press
27500 Drake Rd.
Farmington Hills, MI 48331-3535
Or you can visit our Internet site at gale.cengage.com.

For product information and technology assistance, contact us at:

Gale Customer Support, 1-800-877-4253
For permission to use material from this text or product, submit all requests online at
www.cengage.com/permissions

Further permissions questions can be emailed to permissionrequest@cengage.com

Every effort is made to ensure that Greenhaven Press accurately reflects the original intent of the authors. Every effort has been made to trace the owners of copyrighted material.

Cover image © Peter Marshall/Alamy.
Interior barbed wire artwork © f9photos, used under license from Shutterstock.com.

LIBRARY OF CONGRESS CATALOGING-IN-PUBLICATION DATA

Darfur / Noah Berlatsky, book editor.
    pages cm. -- (Genocide and persecution)
    Includes bibliographical references and index.
    ISBN 978-0-7377-7231-9 (hardcover)
 1. Sudan--History--Darfur Conflict, 2003- 2. Sudan--History--Darfur Conflict, 2003-
--Atrocities. 3. Genocide--Sudan--Darfur. 4. Ethnic conflict--Political aspects--
Sudan--Darfur. 5. Darfur (Sudan)--Ethnic relations--Political aspects. 6. Violence--
Sudan--Darfur. I. Berlatsky, Noah. II. Series: Genocide and persecution.
    DT159.6.D27D3524 2015
    962.704'3--dc23
                                                              2014035142

Printed in the United States of America
1 2 3 4 5 6 7 19 18 17 16 15

Contents

Chapter 1: Historical Background on Mass Atrocities in Darfur

Chapter 2: Controversies Surrounding Mass Atrocities in Darfur

An expert on international justice argues that the arrest warrant for Sudanese president Omar al-Bashir issued by the International Criminal Court should not have been made public and that it fails to make the strongest case possible against al-Bashir.

Chapter 3: Personal Narratives

Preface

*"For the dead and the living, we must
    bear witness."*

> Elie Wiesel, Nobel laureate and
> Holocaust survivor

The histories of many nations are shaped by horrific events involving torture, violent repression, and systematic mass killings. The inhumanity of such events is difficult to comprehend, yet understanding why such events take place, what impact they have on society, and how they may be prevented in the future is vitally important. The Genocide and Persecution series provides readers with anthologies of previously published materials on acts of genocide, crimes against humanity, and other instances of extreme persecution, with an emphasis on events taking place in the twentieth and twenty-first centuries. The series offers essential historical background on these significant events in modern world history, presents the issues and controversies surrounding the events, and provides first-person narratives from people whose lives were altered by the events. By providing primary sources, as well as analysis of crucial issues, these volumes help develop critical-thinking skills and support global connections. In addition, the series directly addresses curriculum standards focused on informational text and literary nonfiction and explicitly promotes literacy in history and social studies.

Each Genocide and Persecution volume focuses on genocide, crimes against humanity, or severe persecution. Material from a variety of primary and secondary sources presents a multinational perspective on the event. Articles are carefully edited and introduced to provide context for readers. The series includes volumes on significant and widely studied events like the Holocaust, as well as events that are less often studied, such as the East Pakistan genocide in what is now Bangladesh. Some volumes focus on multiple events endured by a specific people, such as the Kurds, or multiple events enacted over time by a particular oppressor or in a particular location, such as the People's Republic of China.

Each volume is organized into three chapters. The first chapter provides readers with general background information and uses primary sources such as testimony from tribunals or international courts, documents or speeches from world leaders, and legislative text. The second chapter presents multinational perspectives on issues and controversies and addresses current implications or long-lasting effects of the event. Viewpoints explore such topics as root causes; outside interventions, if any; the impact on the targeted group and the region; and the contentious issues that arose in the aftermath. The third chapter presents first-person narratives from affected people, including survivors, family members of victims, perpetrators, officials, aid workers, and other witnesses.

In addition, numerous features are included in each volume of Genocide and Persecution:

- An annotated **table of contents** provides a brief summary of each essay in the volume.

- A **foreword** gives important background information on the recognition, definition, and study of genocide in recent history and examines current efforts focused on the prevention of future atrocities.

- A **chronology** offers important dates leading up to, during, and following the event.

- **Primary sources**—including historical newspaper accounts, testimony, and personal narratives—are among the varied selections in the anthology.

- **Illustrations**—including a world map, photographs, charts, graphs, statistics, and tables—are closely tied to the text and chosen to help readers understand key points or concepts.

- **Sidebars**—including biographies of key figures and overviews of earlier or related historical events—offer additional content.
- **Pedagogical features**—including analytical exercises, writing prompts, and group activities—introduce each chapter and help reinforce the material. These features promote proficiency in writing, speaking, and listening skills and literacy in history and social studies.
- A **glossary** defines key terms, as needed.
- An annotated list of international **organizations to contact** presents sources of additional information on the volume topic.
- A **list of primary source documents** provides an annotated list of reports, treaties, resolutions, and judicial decisions related to the volume topic.
- A **for further research** section offers a bibliography of books, periodical articles, and Internet sources and an annotated section of other items such as films and websites.
- A comprehensive subject **index** provides access to key people, places, events, and subjects cited in the text.

The Genocide and Persecution series illuminates atrocities that cannot and should not be forgotten. By delving deeply into these events from a variety of perspectives, students and other readers are provided with the information they need to think critically about the past and its implications for the future.

Foreword

The term *genocide* often appears in news stories and other literature. It is not widely known, however, that the core meaning of the term comes from a legal definition, and the concept became part of international criminal law only in 1951 when the United Nations Convention on the Prevention and Punishment of the Crime of Genocide came into force. The word *genocide* appeared in print for the first time in 1944 when Raphael Lemkin, a Polish Jewish refugee from Adolf Hitler's World War II invasion of Eastern Europe, invented the term and explored its meaning in his pioneering book *Axis Rule in Occupied Europe*.

Humanity's Recognition of Genocide and Persecution

Lemkin understood that throughout the history of the human race there have always been leaders who thought they could solve their problems not only through victory in war, but also by destroying entire national, ethnic, racial, or religious groups. Such annihilations of entire groups, in Lemkin's view, deprive the world of the very cultural diversity and richness in languages, traditions, values, and practices that distinguish the human race from all other life on earth. Genocide is not only unjust, it threatens the very existence and progress of human civilization, in Lemkin's eyes.

Looking to the past, Lemkin understood that the prevailing coarseness and brutality of earlier human societies and the lower value placed on human life obscured the existence of genocide. Sacrifice and exploitation, as well as torture and public execution, had been common at different times in history. Looking toward a more humane future, Lemkin asserted the need to punish—and when possible prevent—a crime for which there had been no name until he invented it.

Legal Definitions of Genocide

On December 9, 1948, the United Nations adopted its Convention on the Prevention and Punishment of the Crime of Genocide (UNGC). Under Article II, genocide

> means any of the following acts committed with intent to destroy, in whole or in part, a national, ethnical, racial or religious group, as such:
>
> (a) Killing members of the group;
>
> (b) Causing serious bodily or mental harm to members of the group;
>
> (c) Deliberately inflicting on the group conditions of life calculated to bring about its physical destruction in whole or in part;
>
> (d) Imposing measures intended to prevent births within the group;
>
> (e) Forcibly transferring children of the group to another group.

Article III of the convention defines the elements of the crime of genocide, making punishable:

> (a) Genocide;
>
> (b) Conspiracy to commit genocide;
>
> (c) Direct and public incitement to commit genocide;
>
> (d) Attempt to commit genocide;
>
> (e) Complicity in genocide.

After intense debate, the architects of the convention excluded acts committed with intent to destroy social, political, and economic groups from the definition of genocide. Thus, attempts to destroy whole social classes—the physically and mentally challenged, and homosexuals, for example—are not acts of genocide under the terms of the UNGC. These groups achieved a belated but very significant measure of protection under international criminal law in the Rome Statute of the International Criminal

Court, adopted at a conference on July 17, 1998, and entered into force on July 1, 2002.

The Rome Statute defined a crime against humanity in the following way:

> any of the following acts when committed as part of a widespread and systematic attack directed against any civilian population:
>
> (a) Murder;
>
> (b) Extermination;
>
> (c) Enslavement;
>
> (d) Deportation or forcible transfer of population;
>
> (e) Imprisonment or other severe deprivation of physical liberty in violation of fundamental rules of international law;
>
> (f) Torture;
>
> (g) Rape, sexual slavery, enforced prostitution, forced pregnancy, enforced sterilization, or any other form of sexual violence of comparable gravity;
>
> (h) Persecution against any identifiable group or collectivity on political, racial, national, ethnic, cultural, religious, gender . . . or other grounds that are universally recognized as impermissible under international law, in connection with any act referred to in this paragraph or any crime within the jurisdiction of this Court;
>
> (i) Enforced disappearance of persons;
>
> (j) The crime of apartheid;
>
> (k) Other inhumane acts of a similar character intentionally causing great suffering, or serious injury to body or to mental or physical health.

Although genocide is often ranked as "the crime of crimes," in practice prosecutors find it much easier to convict perpetrators of crimes against humanity rather than genocide under domestic laws. However, while Article I of the UNGC declares that countries adhering to the UNGC recognize genocide as "a crime under international law which they undertake to prevent and to punish," the Rome Statute provides no comparable international mechanism for the prosecution of crimes against humanity. A treaty would help individual countries and international institutions introduce measures to prevent crimes against humanity, as well as open more avenues to the domestic and international prosecution of war criminals.

The Evolving Laws of Genocide

In the aftermath of the serious crimes committed against civilians in the former Yugoslavia since 1991 and the Rwanda genocide of 1994, the United Nations Security Council created special international courts to bring the alleged perpetrators of these events to justice. While the UNGC stands as the standard definition of genocide in law, the new courts contributed significantly to today's nuanced meaning of genocide, crimes against humanity, ethnic cleansing, and serious war crimes in international criminal law.

Also helping to shape contemporary interpretations of such mass atrocity crimes are the special and mixed courts for Sierra Leone, Cambodia, Lebanon, and Iraq, which may be the last of their type in light of the creation of the International Criminal Court (ICC), with its broad jurisdiction over mass atrocity crimes in all countries that adhere to the Rome Statute of the ICC. The Yugoslavia and Rwanda tribunals have already clarified the law of genocide, ruling that rape can be prosecuted as a weapon in committing genocide, evidence of intent can be absent when convicting low-level perpetrators of genocide, and public incitement to commit genocide is a crime even if genocide does not immediately follow the incitement.

Several current controversies about genocide are worth noting and will require more research in the future:

1. Dictators accused of committing genocide or persecution may hold onto power more tightly for fear of becoming

vulnerable to prosecution after they step down. Therefore, do threats of international indictments of these alleged perpetrators actually delay transfers of power to more representative rulers, thereby causing needless suffering?

2. Would the large sum of money spent for international retributive justice be better spent on projects directly benefiting the survivors of genocide and persecution?

3. Can international courts render justice impartially or do they deliver only "victors' justice," that is the application of one set of rules to judge the vanquished and a different and laxer set of rules to judge the victors?

It is important to recognize that the law of genocide is constantly evolving, and scholars searching for the roots and early warning signs of genocide may prefer to use their own definitions of genocide in their work. While the UNGC stands as the standard definition of genocide in law, the debate over its interpretation and application will never end. The ultimate measure of the value of any definition of genocide is its utility for identifying the roots of genocide and preventing future genocides.

Motives for Genocide and Early Warning Signs

When identifying past cases of genocide, many scholars work with some version of the typology of motives published in 1990 by historian Frank Chalk and sociologist Kurt Jonassohn in their book *The History and Sociology of Genocide*. The authors identify the following four motives and acknowledge that they may overlap, or several lesser motives might also drive a perpetrator:

1. To eliminate a real or potential threat, as in Imperial Rome's decision to annihilate Carthage in 146 B.C.

2. To spread terror among real or potential enemies, as in Genghis Khan's destruction of city-states and people who rebelled against the Mongols in the thirteenth century.

3. To acquire economic wealth, as in the case of the Massachusetts Puritans' annihilation of the native Pequot people
   in 1637.
4. To implement a belief, theory, or an ideology, as in the
   case of Germany's decision under Hitler and the Nazis to
   destroy completely the Jewish people of Europe from 1941
   to 1945.

Although these motives represent differing goals, they share
common early warning signs of genocide. A good example of
genocide in recent times that could have been prevented through
close attention to early warning signs was the genocide of 1994 in-
flicted on the people labeled as "Tutsi" in Rwanda. Between 1959
and 1963, the predominantly Hutu political parties in power stig-
matized all Tutsi as members of a hostile racial group, violently
forcing their leaders and many civilians into exile in neighboring
countries through a series of assassinations and massacres. Despite
systematic exclusion of Tutsi from service in the military, government security agencies, and public service, as well as systematic
discrimination against them in higher education, hundreds of
thousands of Tutsi did remain behind in Rwanda. Government-
issued cards identified each Rwandan as Hutu or Tutsi.

A generation later, some Tutsi raised in refugee camps in
Uganda and elsewhere joined together, first organizing politically and then militarily, to reclaim a place in their homeland.
When the predominantly Tutsi Rwanda Patriotic Front invaded
Rwanda from Uganda in October 1990, extremist Hutu political
parties demonized all of Rwanda's Tutsi as traitors, ratcheting up
hate propaganda through radio broadcasts on government-run
Radio Rwanda and privately owned radio station RTLM. Within
the print media, *Kangura* and other publications used vicious car-
toons to further demonize Tutsi and to stigmatize any Hutu who
dared advocate bringing Tutsi into the government. Massacres of
dozens and later hundreds of Tutsi sprang up even as Rwandans
prepared to elect a coalition government led by moderate politi-

cal parties, and as the United Nations dispatched a small international military force led by Canadian general Roméo Dallaire to oversee the elections and political transition. Late in 1992, an international human rights organization's investigating team detected the hate propaganda campaign, verified systematic massacres of Tutsi, and warned the international community that Rwanda had already entered the early stages of genocide, to no avail. On April 6, 1994, Rwanda's genocidal killing accelerated at an alarming pace when someone shot down the airplane flying Rwandan president Juvenal Habyarimana home from peace talks in Arusha, Tanzania.

Hundreds of thousands of Tutsi civilians—including children, women, and the elderly—died horrible deaths because the world ignored the early warning signs of the genocide and refused to act. Prominent among those early warning signs were: 1) systematic, government-decreed discrimination against the Tutsi as members of a supposed racial group; 2) government-issued identity cards labeling every Tutsi as a member of a racial group; 3) hate propaganda casting all Tutsi as subversives and traitors; 4) organized assassinations and massacres targeting Tutsi; and 5) indoctrination of militias and special military units to believe that all Tutsi posed a genocidal threat to the existence of Hutu and would enslave Hutu if they ever again became the rulers of Rwanda.

Genocide Prevention and the Responsibility to Protect

The shock waves emanating from the Rwanda genocide forced world leaders at least to acknowledge in principle that the national sovereignty of offending nations cannot trump the responsibility of those governments to prevent the infliction of mass atrocities on their own people. When governments violate that obligation, the member states of the United Nations have a responsibility to get involved. Such involvement can take the form of, first, offering to help the local government change its ways through technical advice and development aid, and second—if the local government persists in assaulting its own people— initiating armed intervention to protect the civilians at risk. In 2005 the United Nations began to implement the Responsibility to Protect initiative, a framework of principles to guide the international community in preventing mass atrocities.

As in many real-world domains, theory and practice often diverge. Genocide and crimes against humanity are rooted in problems that produce failing states: poverty, poor education, extreme nationalism, lawlessness, dictatorship, and corruption. Implementing the principles of the Responsibility to Protect doctrine burdens intervening state leaders with the necessity of addressing each of those problems over a long period of time. And when those problems prove too intractable and complex to solve easily, the citizens of the intervening nations may lose patience, voting out the leader who initiated the intervention. Arguments based solely on humanitarian principles fail to overcome such concerns. What is needed to persuade political leaders to stop preventable mass atrocities are compelling arguments based on their own national interests.

Preventable mass atrocities threaten the national interests of all states in five specific ways:

1. Mass atrocities create conditions that engender widespread and concrete threats from terrorism, piracy, and other forms of lawlessness on the land and sea;
2. Mass atrocities facilitate the spread of warlordism, whose tentacles block affordable access to vital raw materials produced in the affected country and threaten the prosperity of all nations that depend on the consumption of these resources;
3. Mass atrocities trigger cascades of refugees and internally displaced populations that, combined with climate change and growing international air travel, will accelerate the worldwide incidence of lethal infectious diseases;

4. Mass atrocities spawn single-interest parties and political agendas that drown out more diverse political discourse in the countries where the atrocities take place and in the countries that host large numbers of refugees. Xenophobia and nationalist backlashes are the predictable consequences of government indifference to mass atrocities elsewhere that could have been prevented through early actions;

5. Mass atrocities foster the spread of national and transnational criminal networks trafficking in drugs, women, arms, contraband, and laundered money.

Alerting elected political representatives to the consequences of mass atrocities should be part of every student movement's agenda in the twenty-first century. Adam Smith, the great political economist and author of *The Wealth of Nations*, put it best when he wrote: "It is not from the benevolence of the butcher, the brewer, or the baker that we expect our dinner, but from their regard to their own interest." Self-interest is a powerful engine for good in the marketplace and can be an equally powerful motive and source of inspiration for state action to prevent genocide and mass persecution. In today's new global village, the lives we save may be our own.

Frank Chalk

Frank Chalk, who has a doctorate from the University of Wisconsin–Madison, is a professor of history and director of the Montreal Institute for Genocide and Human Rights Studies at Concordia University in Montreal, Canada. He is coauthor, with Kurt Jonassohn, of The History and Sociology of Genocide *(1990); coauthor, with General Roméo Dallaire, Kyle Matthews, Carla Barqueiro, and Simon Doyle, of* Mobilizing the Will to Intervene: Leadership to Prevent Mass Atrocities *(2010); and associate editor of the three-volume Macmillan Reference USA* Encyclopedia of Genocide and Crimes Against Humanity *(2004). Chalk served as president of the International Association of Genocide Scholars from June 1999 to June 2001. His current research focuses on the use of radio and television broadcasting in the incitement and prevention of genocide, and domestic laws on genocide. For more information on genocide and examples of the experiences of people displaced by genocide and other human rights violations, interested readers can consult the websites of the Montreal Institute for Genocide and Human Rights Studies (http://migs.concordia.ca) and the Montreal Life Stories project (www.lifestoriesmontreal.ca).*

World Map

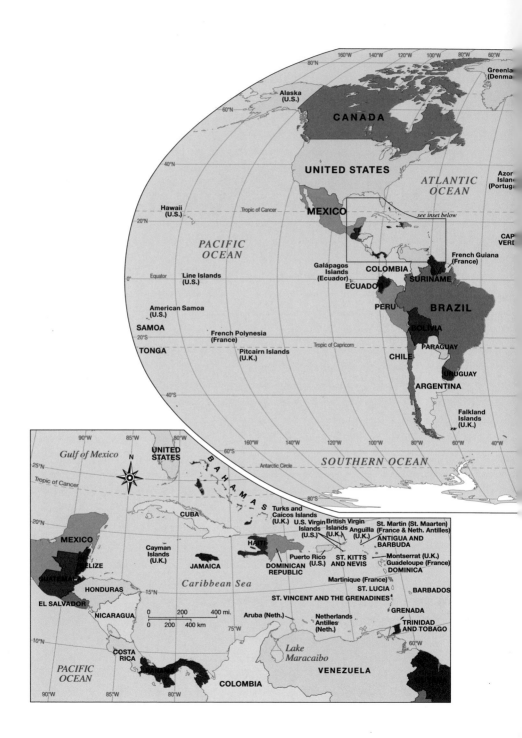

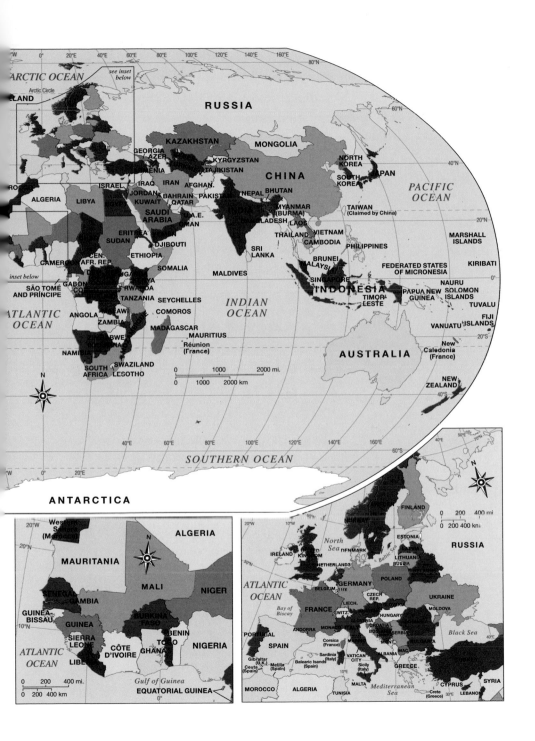

ARCTIC OCEAN

see inset below

Arctic Circle

RUSSIA

KAZAKHSTAN
MONGOLIA

GEORGIA
AZER.
ARMENIA
KYRGYZSTAN
TAJIKISTAN

NORTH KOREA
JAPAN

CHINA
SOUTH KOREA

PACIFIC OCEAN

ISRAEL
IRAN
AFGHAN.
IRAQ

JORDAN
BAHRAIN
PAKISTAN
NEPAL
BHUTAN

ALGERIA
LIBYA
EGYPT
KUWAIT
QATAR

SAUDI ARABIA
U.A.E.
OMAN
INDIA
BANGLADESH

MYANMAR
(BURMA)
LAOS

TAIWAN
(Claimed by China)

ERITREA
YEMEN
THAILAND
VIETNAM
CAMBODIA

MARSHALL ISLANDS

SUDAN
DJIBOUTI
SRI LANKA
PHILIPPINES

KIRIBATI

CAMEROON
CEN. AFR. REP.
ETHIOPIA
SOMALIA
BRUNEI
MALAYSIA
FEDERATED STATES OF MICRONESIA

inset below
GABON
CONGO
MALDIVES
SINGAPORE
NAURU

SÃO TOMÉ AND PRÍNCIPE
KENYA
RWANDA
INDONESIA
TIMOR-LESTE
PAPUA NEW GUINEA
SOLOMON ISLANDS

ATLANTIC OCEAN
TANZANIA
SEYCHELLES
INDIAN OCEAN
TUVALU

ANGOLA
MALAWI
COMOROS
VANUATU
FIJI ISLANDS

ZAMBIA
MADAGASCAR
New Caledonia (France)

NAMIBIA
ZIMBABWE
BOTSWANA
MAURITIUS
Réunion (France)
AUSTRALIA

SOUTH AFRICA
SWAZILAND
LESOTHO
0   1000   2000 mi.
0   1000   2000 km

NEW ZEALAND

SOUTHERN OCEAN

ANTARCTICA

Western Sahara (Morocco)
ALGERIA

MAURITANIA
MALI
NIGER

FINLAND
NORWAY
ESTONIA
RUSSIA

SENEGAL
GAMBIA

North Sea
IRELAND
UNITED KINGDOM
DENMARK
Baltic Sea
LITHUANIA
RUSSIA

GUINEA-BISSAU
GUINEA
BURKINA FASO
BENIN
TOGO
NIGERIA

NETHERLANDS
GERMANY
POLAND
UKRAINE

SIERRA LEONE
CÔTE D'IVOIRE
GHANA

ATLANTIC OCEAN
BELGIUM
LUX.
CZECH REP.
MOLDOVA

ATLANTIC OCEAN
LIBERIA

Bay of Biscay
LIECH.
FRANCE
SWITZ.
HUNGARY

Gulf of Guinea
EQUATORIAL GUINEA

ANDORRA
MONACO
CROATIA
BOS.
SERBIA
Black Sea

PORTUGAL
SPAIN
Corsica (France)
ITALY
MONT.
BULGARIA

Gibraltar (U.K.)
Ceuta (Spain)
Melilla (Spain)
Balearic Isands (Spain)
Sardinia (Italy)
VATICAN CITY
Sicily (Italy)
ALBANIA
MAC.
GREECE

MOROCCO
ALGERIA
TUNISIA
MALTA
Mediterranean Sea
Crete (Greece)
CYPRUS
SYRIA
LEBANON

Chronology

1899	Sudan comes under joint British-Egyptian rule.
1956	Sudan gains independence.
1962	Civil war breaks out between northern Sudan and a southern separatist group called Anya Nya.
1972	Sudanese president Jaafar Numeiri agrees to limited autonomy for southern Sudan.
1978	Oil is discovered in southern Sudan.
1983	President Numeiri abolishes southern autonomy. A second civil war breaks out. The southern rebels—the Sudan People's Liberation Movement (SPLM)—are led by John Garang.
1989	The military, under the leadership of Omar al-Bashir, seizes power in Sudan.
2002	An agreement is signed between North and South Sudan. It provides for a ceasefire and allows for the South to seek independence in six years.
2003	Rebel groups in Darfur take arms against the government, protesting government neglect and oppression of non-Arabs as well as the government practice of arming Arab militias.
2004	The Sudanese government responds to rebellion in Darfur with great force and

arms more militias. Violence escalates, and hundreds of thousands of refugees in Darfur flee the country. Ultimately tens of thousands of civilians are killed. International condemnation of the Sudanese government's actions has little effect, and African Union (AU) peacekeepers are deployed.

2005   The Sudanese government and southern rebels sign an official peace agreement. The Darfur conflict continues, and the United Nations refers the case to the International Criminal Court (ICC).

2006–2008   Violence continues in Darfur, and negotiated peace agreements fail to be accepted by all rebel groups.

2009   The ICC issues an arrest warrant for President al-Bashir for crimes against humanity, the first time such a warrant has been issued for a current head of state. In retaliation, al-Bashir expels a number of humanitarian aid agencies from Darfur.

2011   South Sudan votes to secede and becomes its own nation. A peace agreement between the government of Sudan and rebels in Darfur is signed in Doha, Qatar, but violence continues.

CHAPTER 1

Historical Background on Mass Atrocities in Darfur

Chapter Exercises

1. Analyzing Statistics

Question 1: What is the majority ethnic group in Sudan? Approximately what percentage of the population are ethnic minorities?

Question 2: How much of the land in Sudan is usable for crops? Considering the country's total population, does the amount seem to be sufficient for feeding the people of Sudan?

Question 3: How does the gross domestic product (GDP) of Sudan compare with the rest of the world? Is it a comparatively poor or rich country?

2. Writing Prompt

Write an article about Darfuris displaced by the violence and mass atrocities in Sudan from 2003 to the present day. Give the story a strong title that will capture the audience's attention. Include background that would help your reader understand the reasons for the crisis. Give details that explain the overall crisis and answer who, what, when, where, and why.

3. Group Activity

Break into small groups to discuss the arrest warrant issued for Sudanese president Omar al-Bashir. Did formally accusing al-Bashir of war crimes and crimes against humanity serve or undermine justice? Consider issues such as the known facts about mass killings, attempts at peace negotiations, the evidence against al-Bashir, the purpose and history of the International Criminal Court, and al-Bashir's point of view. Compose a written statement on the group's position in the form of a speech for delivery at the United Nations.

War and Human Rights Abuses Are Reported in Darfur

International Commission of Inquiry on Darfur

The Report of the International Commission of Inquiry on Darfur to the United Nations Secretary General documents the official findings of an investigation commissioned by the United Nations. The report says that there is evidence that government-backed Arab militias in Darfur attacked and massacred civilians on the basis of ethnicity. There is also lesser evidence of atrocities by rebel groups in the region. The report concludes that evidence of genocide—the effort to exterminate an entire people—is uncertain.

182. In accordance with its mandate set out by the Security Council, requesting the Commission to "investigate reports of violations of human rights law and international humanitarian law", the Commission carefully studied reports from different sources including Governments, inter-governmental organizations, various United Nations mechanisms or bodies, as well as non-governmental organizations. Immediately following the establishment of the Commission, a *Note Verbale* [diplomatic communication] was sent out to Member States and international and regional organizations on 28 October 2004, requesting that

any relevant information be submitted to the Commission. A similar letter was sent to non-governmental organizations on 2 November 2004. The Commission subsequently received a great number of documents and other material from a wide variety of sources, including the Government of the Sudan. These materials were organized in a database and analyzed by the Commission. The following is a brief account of these reports, which serves to clarify the context of the fact finding and the investigations conducted by the Commission. In the sections following this overview, individual incidents are presented according to the type of violation or international crime identified.

Violations of International Human Rights and Humanitarian Law

183. Information presented in the earlier reports examined by the Commission is mainly based on witness accounts compiled through interviews of IDPs [internally displaced persons] and refugees. Some of the later reports are based on a broader inquiry drawing from other sources and methods to gather information, including satellite imagery to detect destruction and burning of villages as well as field visits to Darfur itself. These reports have also relied upon findings of researchers and observers from different organizations monitoring the situation in Darfur.

184. Most reports note a pattern of indiscriminate attacks on civilians in villages and communities in all three Darfur states beginning in early 2003. Attacks also took place in 2001 and 2002, however, the magnitude, intensity and consistency of the attacks increased noticeably beginning in early 2003. It is generally agreed that this escalation coincides with the intensification of the internal armed conflict between the Government and the two rebel movements, the Sudan Liberation Movement/Army (SLM/A) and the Justice and Equality Movement (JEM). A large part of the information relates to the impact of this conflict on

the civilian population, including reference to the methods of combat employed by the parties, and the counter-insurgency policies of the Government.

Attacks Against Civilians

185. A common conclusion is that, in its response to the insurgency, the Government has committed acts against the civilian population, directly or through surrogate armed groups, which amount to gross violations of human rights and humanitarian law. While there has been comparatively less information on violations committed by the rebel groups, some sources have reported incidents of such violations. There is also information that indicates activities of armed elements who have taken advantage of the total collapse of law and order to settle scores in the context of traditional tribal feuds, or to simply loot and raid livestock.

186. There are consistent accounts of a recurrent pattern of attacks on villages and settlements, sometimes involving aerial attacks by helicopter gunships or fixed-wing aircraft (Antonov and MIG), including bombing and strafing with automatic weapons. However, a majority of the attacks reported are ground assaults by the military, the Janjaweed, or a combination of the two. Hundreds of incidents have been reported involving the killing of civilians, massacres, summary executions, rape and other forms of sexual violence, torture, abduction, looting of property and livestock, as well as deliberate destruction and torching of villages. These incidents have resulted in the massive displacement of large parts of the civilian population within Darfur as well as to neighbouring Chad. The reports indicate that the intensity of the attacks and the atrocities committed in any one village spread such a level of fear that populations from surrounding villages that escaped such attacks also fled to areas of relative security.

187. Except in a few cases, these incidents are reported to have occurred without any military justification in relation to any specific activity of the rebel forces. This has strengthened the general perception amongst observers that the civilian population has been knowingly and deliberately targeted to achieve common or specific objectives and interests of the Government and the Janjaweed.

188. Eye-witness accounts of many incidents published in these reports mention that the assailant forces are in uniform, but make a distinction between the uniforms worn by the regular military and the Janjaweed. A variety of explanations have been offered for this distinction in the reports, including that the Government's Popular Defence Forces (PDF), largely recruited from within the Arab tribes, are included in the term "Janjaweed" as it is commonly used in the context of this conflict. Others allege

A Sudanese rebel fighter from the Justice and Equality Movement (JEM) watches the abandoned village of Chero Kasi burn after Janjaweed militiamen set it ablaze in 2004. Hundreds of villages were burned to the ground, making them uninhabitable. © Scott Nelson/ Getty Images.

that the Government provides the militia with these uniforms as well as weapons and see this as a confirmation of their affiliation and association with the Government.

189. Some reports also contain accounts of military engagements between Government and rebel forces which have resulted in severe violations of the rights of civilian populations, and which demonstrate a complete disregard by the warring parties for their obligations regarding the security of civilians. It is reported that wanton acts of destruction, far exceeding any military imperative, were committed, mostly by Government forces. Janjaweed have featured in some of these incidents contributing to the destruction, particularly by inflicting harm on civilian populations and through wide scale looting in the course of, or following, the battle.

Most Attacks Attributed to the Government and the Janjaweed

190. Although there is little information on violations committed by the *rebel forces*, there are some reports that they have engaged in indiscriminate attacks resulting in civilian deaths and injuries and destruction of private property. There are further reports of the killing of wounded and imprisoned soldiers, attacking or launching attacks from protected buildings such as hospitals, abduction of civilians and humanitarian workers, enforced disappearances of Government officials, [and] looting of livestock, commercial vehicles and goods. There are also allegations of the use of child soldiers by the rebels. However, it should be noted that the number of reported violations allegedly committed by the Government forces and the Janjaweed by far exceeds the number of cases reported on rebels.

191. While a majority of the reports are consistent in the description of events and the violations committed, the crimes

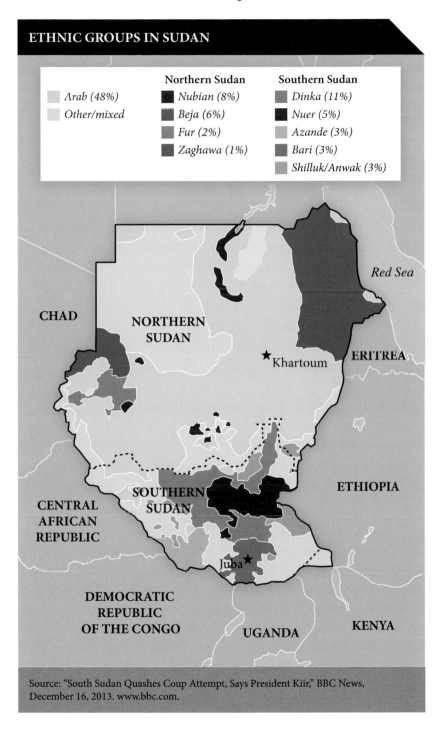

ETHNIC GROUPS IN SUDAN

	Northern Sudan	Southern Sudan
Arab (48%)	Nubian (8%)	Dinka (11%)
Other/mixed	Beja (6%)	Nuer (5%)
	Fur (2%)	Azande (3%)
	Zaghawa (1%)	Bari (3%)
		Shilluk/Anwak (3%)

CHAD

NORTHERN
SUDAN

Red Sea

★ Khartoum

ERITREA

ETHIOPIA

CENTRAL
AFRICAN
REPUBLIC

SOUTHERN
SUDAN

Juba ★

DEMOCRATIC
REPUBLIC
OF THE CONGO

UGANDA

KENYA

Source: "South Sudan Quashes Coup Attempt, Says President Kiir," BBC News,
December 16, 2013. www.bbc.com.

attributed to the Government forces and Janjaweed have varied according to the differences in the interpretation of the events and the context in which they have occurred. Analyses of facts by most of the observers, nevertheless, suggest that the most serious violations of human rights and humanitarian law have been committed by militias, popularly termed "Janjaweed", at the behest of and with the complicity of the Government, which recruited these elements as a part of its counterinsurgency campaign.

192. Various reports and the media claim to have convincing evidence that areas have been specifically targeted because of the proximity to or the *locus* of rebel activity, but more importantly because of the ethnic composition of the population that inhabits these areas. Almost all entities that have reported on the situation in Darfur have noted that the populations subjected to violations are Darfurians who identify themselves as Africans, distinguishable from the Arab tribes in the region, which are also reported to constitute the majority of the Janjaweed.

Ethnic and Tribal Populations Targeted

193. It is reported that amongst the African tribes, members of the Zaghawa, Fur and Masaalit tribes, which have a marked concentration of population in some areas, have been particularly targeted. This is generally attributed to the fact that the two main rebel groups in Darfur are ethnically African and are largely drawn from these three tribes. It is for this reason that some observers have concluded that a major objective of destruction and depopulation of targeted areas is to eliminate or pre-empt any possibility of support for the rebels.

194. Some reports take into account the historical context of ethnic and tribal politics in Darfur, and differences in the way of life and means of livelihood that have resulted in competing claims over control and utilization of natural resources and land.

On this basis, some reports conclude that elements of persecution and "ethnic cleansing" are present in the pattern of destruction and displacement.

195. This reading of the information by some sources has given an added dimension to the conflict. Reports of deliberate destruction of the very means of survival of these populations have been seen as a design towards their permanent expulsion from their places of habitation. Many of the sources have suggested that the acts of killings, destruction and forced displacement, taken as a whole, amount to extermination. Some reports have implied, and a few have determined, that the elements of the crime of genocide are present in the patterns and nature of violations committed by the Government and its militias.

Concerns About the Displaced Population

196. According to recent reports, even though military offensives and large-scale displacement of civilians in North and West Darfur have diminished in the past few months, probably because large parts of the rural areas under Government control have been emptied of their rural inhabitants, violence there has not ceased. In Government-controlled areas, displaced civilians have remained largely at the mercy of the Janjaweed. Observers have reported that displaced civilians living under Government control in these areas remain virtual prisoners—confined to camps and settlements with inadequate food, shelter and humanitarian assistance, at constant risk of further attacks, rape and looting of their remaining possessions. Even if incidents are reported to the police or other Government officials, little or no action is taken to arrest perpetrators. Government-backed Janjaweed raids on new areas in South Darfur have also been reported. There have also been reports of unidentified "militia incursions" along the border into Chad, often with the apparent aim of raiding cattle and other livestock.

197. Concerns have been expressed that despite the Government's assurances to the international community, the security situation has not improved. Most IDPs remain afraid to return to their places of origin out of fear of renewed attacks and due to the prevailing situation of impunity for acts of violence committed against the civilian population. Some more recent reports note that Arab populations have begun to settle in a few areas previously occupied by the displaced populations.

198. One report noted that the situation in Darfur was being distorted by international organizations and international media. According to this source, the humanitarian situation was being blown out of proportion by most observers. The cause of the conflict should be mainly ascribed to tribal animosities, while the Government had responded to a rebellion and was also providing humanitarian assistance to the displaced and affected populations.

Powell Calls Sudan Killings Genocide

CNN.com

In the following viewpoint, CNN reports on the decision by US secretary of state Colin Powell to declare the violence in Darfur a genocide. The report says that the label "genocide" triggers no particular legal consequences, but lays the groundwork for potential action in the future. The report also notes that both the United Nations and the United States have called for the Sudanese government to end the violence in Darfur.

U.S. Secretary of State Colin Powell said Thursday [September 9, 2004] that "genocide has been committed" in the Sudanese region of Darfur.

Powell cited a "consistent and widespread" pattern of atrocities—including killings, rapes and burning of villages.

"This was a coordinated effort, not just random violence," he said.

Powell, who recently visited Sudan, was speaking to the Senate Foreign Relations Committee.

An international law expert said the statement does not require the United States to act, but establishes a basis for it to intervene under international law.

"That Powell has said this is politically significant," said Hurst Hannum, professor of international law at the Fletcher School at Tufts University in Boston. "It doesn't trigger any legal consequences . . . (but) there will certainly be more of a push for something to be done."

Secretary of State Colin Powell (center) is escorted through a Sudanese refugee camp in 2004. © AP Photo/Department of State.

US Confusion on Darfur

President Bush had made a great show of pushing for economic sanctions on Sudan, but when the Darfur Peace and Accountability Act came close to being voted [on] in Congress (September 2006), he instructed Republican Senators to block it because the US Securities and Exchange Commission was against it. In 2005, while debate raged about the probable death toll in Darfur, . . . Bob Zoellick got the State Department to declassify an inane report putting the total casualties at between 60,000 and 140,000. This did not stop President Bush from asking a few months later for "a NATO stewardship in Darfur", a move that was almost immediately contradicted by Bush's own UN Ambassador John Bolton, who said that there would be no US forces sent to Darfur—NATO or no NATO—while in Brussels Jaap de Hoop Scheffer, NATO's Secretary General, said he had received no official US demand for a NATO intervention. The US administration could not even synchronize on whether it should call Darfur a genocide or not. In the early days of the crisis Secretary of State Colin Powell had called Darfur "a genocide" and so had President Bush himself. But on 10 October 2005 Ambassador Bolton had prevented Juan Mendez, Kofi Annan's Special Advisor for the Prevention of Genocide, from giving a briefing on Darfur to the UN, and Under-Secretary of State for Africa Jendayi Frazer had declared that Darfur was "not a genocide but a series of small attacks and incidents". Six months later, after pushing for the vote of UN Resolution 1706, Ambassador Bolton changed tack again and called Darfur a genocide.

Gérard Prunier, Darfur: A 21st Century Genocide, third edition. Ithaca, NY: Cornell University Press, 2008, p. 183.

Arab Janjaweed militias have been accused of committing widespread atrocities against black villagers and displacing hundreds of thousands of people from their homes in the huge African nation.

"The government of Sudan and the Janjaweed bear responsibility," Powell said.

He made his comments as the U.N. Security Council prepared to meet on the matter and study a new draft resolution being circulated by the United States.

The Security Council also will discuss a report on the problem U.N. Secretary-General Kofi Annan prepared last week.

U.N. Resolution on Darfur

The draft resolution, put on the table Wednesday [September 8, 2004], says the Sudanese government "has failed fully to comply with its commitments" since the last resolution.

"The situation in Sudan constitutes a threat to international peace and security and to stability in the region," the resolution says.

It also demands that Khartoum stop the violence, cease military flights over Darfur, and increase access to international aid. It also calls for a larger monitoring force.

On July 30, the Security Council passed a resolution threatening action against Khartoum if it failed to disarm the Janjaweed militias and restore security within 30 days. That deadline recently passed.

The conflict in Darfur, in western Sudan, began last year when black Sudanese rebels attacked government property, accusing the government of neglecting Darfur in favor of the Arab population in Sudan.

The government responded by sending the Janjaweed to put down the rebellion in Darfur. The warring factions recently agreed to a cease-fire, but violence between them has continued.

Several international human rights groups estimate that 15,000 to 30,000 civilians have died in Darfur since fighting broke out in February 2003.

More than a million people have been displaced by the hostilities, fleeing to other places in Sudan or across the border to Chad.

Talks are continuing in the Nigerian capital of Abuja to "resolve the political dispute driving the conflict," the United Nations said.

Refugees Talk of Destruction

Powell's assessment is based in large part on interviews in Chad of more than 1,100 Darfur refugees—a project undertaken by the State Department to determine whether the atrocities committed against Darfur's black Africans were racially motivated.

Powell said three-fourths of those interviewed said "Sudanese military forces were involved in the attack" and "villages often experienced multiple attacks over a prolonged period before they were destroyed by burning, shelling or bombing, making it impossible for villagers to return."

He said Janjaweed and Sudanese forces also "destroyed villages' foodstuffs and other means of survival" and "obstructed food, water, medicine and other humanitarian aid."

The government failed to halt the onslaught "despite having been put on notice multiple times," he said.

Officials have said the findings are consistent with reports from human rights groups that have visited the region.

Yet, the Sudanese government has denied that what has taken place in Darfur is genocide.

And Powell said he doubts Sudan will agree now that there is genocide in the region, but he believes it should heed the United States' findings.

"The Sudanese government and the Sudanese legislature will reflect on what I have said here today and on what I hope the international community will say in the next resolution.

"We are not after Sudan, we are not trying to punish the people or the Sudanese government. We are trying to save lives."

The U.N.'s Genocide Convention, unlike other human rights treaties, does not establish a specific monitoring body or expert committee to respond to genocide.

It does say that the United Nations can take up the matter and consider the necessary approach "for the prevention and suppression of acts of genocide."

How Genocide Is Defined

Powell described the three criteria used to identify genocide under the Genocide Convention:

- Specific acts are committed—killing, causing serious bodily or mental harm, deliberately inflicting conditions of life calculated to bring about physical destruction of a group in whole or in part, imposing measures to prevent births or forcibly transferring children to another group;
- Such acts are committed against members of a national, ethnic, racial or religious group, and;
- Such acts are carried out "with intent to destroy, in whole or in part, [the group] as such."

"Sudan is a contracting party to the Genocide Convention and is obliged under the convention to prevent and punish acts of genocide," Powell said.

At this time, he said, "it appears Sudan has failed to do so."

"Today we are calling on the United Nations to initiate a full investigation" into genocide, Powell said.

He said he hopes that the next Security Council resolution into Sudan requests an investigation into all violations of human rights law in the country.

"The evidence leads us to the conclusion that genocide has occurred and may still be occurring in Darfur."

Israel to Block New Refugees from Darfur

Ellen Knickmeyer

Ellen Knickmeyer is a former Associated Press bureau chief for West Africa and Washington Post *bureau chief for Baghdad and Cairo. In the following viewpoint, she reports on the efforts of refugees from the violence in Darfur to cross from Egypt into Israel. Israel has refused to receive most of them and returned them to Egypt, where many of them will be returned to Darfur and face violence and reprisals for dealing with Israel. Knickmeyer says the decision to expel the refugees is controversial within Israel for humanitarian and legal reasons.*

Israel closed the door Sunday [August 2007] on a surge of asylum-seekers from Sudan's Darfur region and from other African countries, the largest influx of non-Jewish refugees in the modern history of the Jewish state.

Authorities announced that they had expelled 48 of more than 2,000 African refugees who have entered illegally from Egypt in recent weeks. Officials said they would allow 500

Darfurians among them to remain, but would deport everyone else back to Egypt and accept no more illegal migrants from Darfur or other places.

The announcement, raising new concerns over the refugees' safety, heightened a debate in Israel over what responsibilities a nation created by survivors of genocide in Europe bore toward people fleeing mass killing in Africa.

It was unclear Sunday whether Egypt would in turn deport the refugees to their countries of origin. Israel had received assurances from Egypt that it would not send Sudanese refugees to their troubled home country, an Israeli official said by telephone, speaking on condition of anonymity.

Egyptian police told the Associated Press, however, that Egypt would send the Sudanese back to Sudan. An Egyptian Foreign Ministry official, also speaking on condition of anonymity, said Israel had sought no assurances about the future of the refugees. "Israel just said, 'Please take them,'" the Egyptian official said.

Escaping Genocide in Sudan

Refugees from Darfur are escaping what President Bush and others have called genocide by government-allied Arab militias against ethnic African villagers. In addition, Sudan and Israel officially are enemies, and Sudan's government has said any refugees sent back from Israel would be considered as having dealt with an enemy state and treated accordingly.

"If deported to Sudan, they will be tried for treason," said Madhal Aguer, a private aid worker in Cairo for refugees from a separate conflict in southern Sudan; a long-running civil war between the north and south killed up to 1 million people before a peace deal in 2005.

Since the 1990s, more than 2 million Sudanese have fled across their country's northern border into Egypt. Although Egypt has generally allowed them to stay, they have faced discrimination and sometimes deadly abuse, and say they find few jobs and little help from refugee agencies.

Refugees from the Darfur region clash with Egyptian police outside the UN refugee headquarters in Cairo in 2004. Refugees faced an uncertain future and feared being returned to Sudan. © AP Photo/Hasan Jamali.

In 2005, Egyptian police used clubs and water cannons to break up a sit-in by Sudanese refugees near the U.N. refugee agency. At least 20 were trampled to death or otherwise killed in the resulting melee, according to health officials and rights workers.

This spring, thousands of the refugees started moving north to sneak into Israel, in the belief it would allow them safety, freedom and jobs, the refugees said. Israel, which normally gets 700 to 800 asylum-seekers a year, received 2,300 in the first six months of the year, said Anat Ben-Dor, a lawyer at a Tel Aviv University legal clinic who represents some of the African refugees.

Nearly all of the new asylum-seekers are from Africa, including about 1,600 from Sudan, according to Israeli figures. Israel has confined some of the arrivals in prisons or in tent cities and trailer camps in the desert, and others in remote kibbutzim.

The Reaction in Egypt

The Africans have generally crossed into Israel over Egypt's Sinai border. Most sell all their goods to pay the $300 to $400 fee demanded by local Bedouin guides. The danger is high; since July, Egyptian authorities have fatally shot at least one refugee, a 28-year-old Darfurian woman, at the border, and shot and wounded several others.

Egypt has sent before military tribunals about 50 refugees caught while trying to cross the border, sentencing them to up to a year in prison. The Egyptian Foreign Ministry official said Sunday that Egypt was holding the refugees expelled this weekend for questioning, but did not intend to try them.

Israeli Prime Minister Ehud Olmert said earlier this summer that Darfurians among the refugees would be absorbed into Israeli society. Government spokesman David Baker said Sunday that Israel would give some members of that group special treatment. "Israel is certainly aware of the unique and dire situation of these refugees from Darfur, and it is based on our humanitarian concerns that we've decided to take in 500 Darfur refugees," Baker said by telephone.

"Regarding those who in the future" are "coming from anywhere . . . they will be sent back to Egypt. That would include anyone coming from Darfur," Baker said.

Disagreements Within the Israeli Government

Israel sent back the first group of 48 African refugees through the Karm Abu Salim, or Kerem Shalom, crossing with Egypt late Saturday night, Egyptian and Israeli officials confirmed. Egypt said the deportees included refugees from Darfur.

Israel apparently expelled them without hearings, in contravention of a refugee accord it has signed that requires countries to determine whether deportation will subject asylum-seekers to mistreatment, said Ben-Dor, the Israeli refugee lawyer.

More than half the members of Israel's parliament, including opposition leader Binyamin Netanyahu, signed a petition earlier this month urging Israel not to send the refugees back to Egypt.

"The refugees need protection and sanctuary and the Jewish people's history as well as democratic and humanitarian values make it a moral imperative for us to give them that shelter," the Israeli lawmakers wrote.

"The expulsion is an inhumane act that violates international law," said lawmaker Dov Khenin of the Hadash party, according to the *Haaretz* newspaper website.

Israel's previous largest influx of non-Jewish refugees came in the late 1970s, when nearly 400 Vietnamese boat people arrived legally under U.N. auspices. This summer's influx was far larger, Ben-Dor noted.

The ICC Issues an Arrest Warrant Against the President of Sudan

Xan Rice

Xan Rice is the East Africa correspondent for The Guardian. *In the following viewpoint, he reports on the decision of the International Criminal Court to charge Sudanese president Omar al-Bashir with war crimes. Rice says that there is much evidence of al-Bashir's participation in the atrocities in Darfur. He also reports that Western powers support the charges, while Arab and African groups fear that the charges will lead to instability in Sudan and may cause al-Bashir to retaliate against opposition groups.*

The Sudanese president, Omar al-Bashir, has been charged with war crimes over the conflict in Darfur, becoming the first sitting head of state issued with an arrest warrant by the International Criminal Court (ICC).

The court, based in The Hague [The Netherlands], upheld the request of the chief prosecutor, Luis Moreno-Ocampo, to charge Bashir with war crimes and crimes against humanity. More than 200,000 people have died since 2003 in the country's western Darfur region.

Judges dismissed the prosecution's most contentious charge of genocide. Prosecutors had alleged Bashir tried to wipe out three non-Arab ethnic groups.

Strong Reactions for and Against the Indictment

Within minutes of the announcement, hundreds of protesters took to the streets in Khartoum, the Sudanese capital.

Mustafa Osman Ismail, an aide to Bashir, described the decision as "neo-colonialism. . . . They do not want Sudan to become stable."

The ICC spokeswoman, Laurence Blairon, said the indictment, drawn up by three judges, included five counts of crimes against humanity: murder, extermination, forcible transfer, torture and rape. The two counts of war crimes were for directing attacks on the civilian population and pillaging.

Blairon said Bashir was criminally responsible as the head of state and commander of the Sudanese armed forces for the offences during a five-year counter-insurgency campaign against three armed groups in Darfur.

She said all states would be asked to execute the arrest warrant and if Sudan failed to cooperate the matter would be referred to the UN Security Council.

Human rights groups hailed the ICC decision to pursue Bashir, who is accused of ordering mass murder, rape and torture in Darfur.

"This sends a strong signal that the international community no longer tolerates impunity for grave violations of human rights committed by people in positions of power," said Tawanda Hondora, the deputy director of Amnesty International's Africa programme.

Bashir Remains Defiant

Sudan does not recognise the ICC, and Bashir yesterday said the court could "eat" the arrest warrant, which he described as a Western plot to hinder Sudan's development.

Despite his defiance, the court's decision will raise immediate questions over his political future and he will find it difficult to travel abroad without the risk of arrest.

The case is by far the biggest and most controversial that the ICC, which started work as a permanent court in 2002, has taken on.

Bashir, who is 65 and has held power for 20 years, joins the likes of the former Liberian president Charles Taylor and the late Yugoslavian leader Slobodan Milosevic, who were indicted by special international tribunals while still in office.

Both were subsequently forced from power and put on trial in The Hague.

A JEM rebel fighter shows scars and missing fingers after a 2004 Janjaweed attack on his village. People who survived such attacks were often left with serious injuries. © Scott Nelson/ Getty Images.

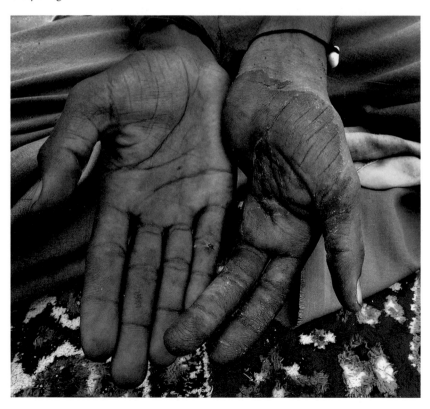

Bashir's Role in the Crisis

Few independent observers doubt Bashir's large share of responsibility for the humanitarian catastrophe in Darfur.

After the uprising in February 2003 by mainly non-Arab rebels, who complained of marginalisation and neglect, his government armed, trained and financed bands of Arab nomads to attack villages across Darfur, killing, raping and looting as they went. The army provided air and ground support.

Moreno-Ocampo says the strategy caused 35,000 violent deaths, and alleges that Bashir wanted to eliminate the Fur, Marsalit and Zaghawa ethnic groups, whom he deemed supportive of the rebels.

"More than 30 witnesses will [testify] how he [Bashir] managed to control everything, and we have strong evidence of his intention," Moreno-Ocampo said yesterday.

But some Sudan experts were not convinced by the genocide charge, which is normally extremely difficult to prove. Equally contentious was the decision to pursue Bashir while he still heads an unpredictable regime in an unstable country.

Mixed International Reactions

The US, UK and France were in favour of the arrest warrant, and hope it may push Sudan's government towards reforms and ending the six-year conflict.

But Arab states and the African Union had pressed for a postponement of the charges to allow Bashir a final chance to end the Darfur conflict while not under duress.

Under the ICC statute, the United Nations can still pass a resolution to defer the prosecution for 12 months, but this seems unlikely given the stance of leading Western powers.

Street protests against the ICC decision are expected in Khartoum, but the government has insisted there will be no impact on national policies.

Some observers fear, however, that Bashir will crack down on opposition groups in the coming months if he feels his power is at stake, and that the 2005 peace deal to end the civil war in the south could also be in peril.

The UN, aid agencies and Western embassies have made emergency plans in case of violence against foreigners.

Neither All-Out War Nor a Proper Peace

The Economist

The Economist is a weekly news magazine based in London. In the following viewpoint, the magazine reports on ongoing violence in Darfur in 2009. The viewpoint notes that the violence has changed in character as the warring armies have factionalized and turned into little more than roving gangs of bandits. Because of the number of groups involved and the lack of a unifying political goal, negotiating peace is very difficult. The viewpoint argues that the United Nations and the African Union could do more to promote peace.

When General Martin Agwai, the outgoing commander of the United Nations and African Union (AU) peacekeeping mission in Darfur, known as UNAMID, said that the war in Sudan's western region had all but dried up, he stirred controversy. Some people are loth to acknowledge that the nature and scale of the violence in Darfur have changed. All the same, violence still rages—and the UN must share the blame for failing to do more to stop it.

Sudan's Civil Wars

The First Sudanese Civil War was fought over regional southern autonomy. At independence, the south was promised federalism. However, the vision of a federal Sudan remained unfulfilled, resulting in almost no political power for the south. The central political powers also have done little to tackle the dismal economic and developmental situation of most Sudanese. The ensuing war killed five hundred thousand people and displaced hundreds of thousands more. Peace negotiations began in 1971 when various southern guerrilla groups formed an alliance as the Southern Sudan Liberation Movement (SSLM) to become a unified negotiation partner to the north. The war officially ended with the signing of the Addis Ababa Agreement in 1972, granting the south regional autonomy and a distinct southern administrative region. In spite of this effort, the agreement failed to establish a peaceful Sudan due to the lack of political will in Khartoum to implement peace. In addition, disunity amongst southern politicians and the absence of a peace dividend for most Sudanese brought the country back to war in 1983. The Second Sudanese Civil War is often seen as a continuation of the first, rather than a distinct war, as there was essentially a contestation over the same issues. In addition, the large and lucrative oil-

In part, the general was stating the obvious. About 300,000 people have died in Darfur as a result of the violence that erupted in 2003 after rebels attacked Sudanese government forces. This year, by contrast, more people have died in inter-ethnic fighting in the south Sudanese state of Jonglei alone than in Darfur, where big clashes have been happening only rarely. The death rate in Darfur, a controversial measure, is widely accepted to be below what aid agencies consider the threshold for an emergency. Especially in America, campaigners who say that genocide is still taking place in Darfur find this hard to admit.

But General Agwai accepted that there was still no peace in Darfur. If anything, the fragmentation of rebel groups, some-

fields in southern Sudan make Khartoum even less likely to truly grant regional autonomy.

The second war was fought between the central government, which in 1989 became an Islamist government after a coup led by Omar Ahmed el-Bashir (b. 1944) and the newly established Sudan People's Liberation Army/Movement (SPLA/M) under Dr. John Garang de Mabior (1945–2005). It was one of Africa's and the world's longest conflicts. Estimates of deaths are commonly in excess of two million, the majority being civilians who died of war-related diseases or malnutrition. Twice as many people were displaced. The SPLA itself, although successful as a fighting force in control of large areas and even oilfields, was struggling with inner conflict. This eventually caused a split and an attempt by Garang's former comrades to overthrow him. That division led to some of the fiercest fighting of the war, which drew on and fuelled long-standing ethnic tensions. Various attempts at peace proved futile for over a decade until the Inter-Governmental Authority on Development (IGAD) peace process led to the signing of the Comprehensive Peace Agreement (CPA) in January 2005.

"Sudan: Wars," New Encyclopedia of Africa, eds. John Middleton and Joseph C. Miller, second edition, vol. 4. Detroit: Charles Scribner's Sons, 2008, pp. 538–541.

times into little more than gangs of bandits, has left it as dangerous as ever—and less predictable. Aid workers and food convoys are often attacked. Low-level fighting is still creating refugees, who must join the 2.7m others in the camps that litter Darfur. UNAMID has failed to stem this violence.

For sure, General Agwai's task has been hampered by circumstances beyond his control. His force arrived at the start of last year but is still less than three-quarters of its mandated strength of 26,000 soldiers and police, the largest such UN peacekeeping force ever deployed. The general also got less logistical support than he wanted. He asked for 18 military helicopters, which are vital in the remote desert region of Darfur, the size of France. So

A United Nations peacekeeper patrols a market at a refugee camp in South Darfur in 2010. The peacekeepers have been accused of not doing enough to promote peace. © Ashraf Shazly/ AFP/Getty Images.

far he has received none. He also faced concerted bureaucratic obstruction by Sudan's government.

Yet UNAMID had substantial assets at its disposal. But it rarely intervenes to stop the fighting. It has done a bit to boost security in Darfur's towns but has provided almost no protection in rural areas. Even in towns, security has been patchy. On August 29th two UNAMID people were kidnapped in Zalingei. "If they can't handle their own security, how can they protect anyone else?" asked one aid worker.

The political head of UNAMID, Rodolphe Adada, a bow-tied Congolese diplomat who also stepped down last week, has been largely ineffective. Others have taken the lead in trying to revive peace talks in Darfur, stalled since the total failure of a conference in Libya in October 2007. On behalf of the AU, Thabo Mbeki, a former South African president, is looking at ways, perhaps involving so-called hybrid courts, to prosecute those responsible for war crimes in Darfur.

The idea is to present an alternative legal framework that Sudan's government might find more palatable than seeing some of its members hauled off to the International Criminal Court (ICC) at The Hague, which has indicted President Omar al-Bashir and two of his top men. Mr Mbeki is expected to report back to the AU later this month. A compromise over the ICC wrangle might possibly let Sudan's government be more willing to make concessions that could lead to a political settlement in Darfur.

At the same time, a variety of other mediators, including the Qataris and a new American special envoy to Sudan, Scott Gration, have been encouraging the disparate rebel groups to resolve their differences and form a more coherent negotiating body. This requires patience. The utter fragmentation of the rebels into warring factions in the past three years is a big reason for the lack of progress towards peace in Darfur. But diplomats are now shuttling between the capitals of Egypt, Libya, Qatar, Sudan and elsewhere. Previous efforts have got nowhere. Recently there has been at least a little spurt of hope.

The Humanitarian Situation in Darfur

IRIN

IRIN is a United Nations (UN) news agency focused on humanitarian issues. In the following viewpoint, IRIN describes ongoing violence and chaos in Darfur. Fighting is no longer between Arabs and blacks, the author states, but has spiraled into conflicts between many different ethnic groups. Rampant banditry has made it impossible for aid agencies to function safely, especially since the Sudanese government actively opposes UN efforts. Violence appears to be worsening, and IRIN concludes that peace efforts seem stalled and not promising.

The UN estimates that the conflict in Sudan's Darfur region has seen some 300,000 people displaced so far in 2013—twice as many as in 2011 and 2012, according to the UN Office for the Coordination of Humanitarian Affairs (OCHA).

"Darfur has seen a new wave of fighting in many areas in 2013. More than 300,000 people have had to flee their homes to escape violence since the beginning of the year, including over 35,000 people who have crossed the borders into Chad and the Central African Republic. The crisis is getting bigger," Mark Cutts, OCHA head of office in Sudan, told IRIN.

The new dimension is localized clashes between Arab communities over gold-mining rights and access to grazing land.

IRIN looks at the humanitarian situation in Darfur, where an estimated 2.3 million people have been displaced by a decade of conflict and insecurity.

What Is the Humanitarian Situation Like?

UN agency figures indicate there are 1.4 million people living in the main camps in Sudan's Darfur region.

Cutts, however, told IRIN that the "actual numbers of IDPs [internally displaced persons] in camps are significantly higher as many of the IDPs living in smaller camps/settlements are not included in these figures and many IDPs in the bigger camps remain unregistered."

A Nigerian member of the police unit of the African Union/UN operation in Darfur (UNAMID) inspects a blood-streaked vehicle in Geneina, Sudan, on October 15, 2013. Seven peacekeepers were killed there in an ambush in July 2013. © AP Photo/Albert Gonzalez Farran, UNAMID.

Many of those affected by the conflict are unable to receive any humanitarian assistance as insecurity has hampered efforts by aid workers to reach them. In total, 3.2 million people—more than a third of Darfur's population—are in need of humanitarian assistance in Darfur.

"Road insecurity remains a major problem affecting movement of humanitarian staff and supplies in Central Darfur. The problem has been compounded by recent increased clashes between Misseriya and Salamat tribesmen in different parts of Central Darfur, as well as the reported movement of armed groups in the state," OCHA said in a recent bulletin.

A recent survey by Médecins Sans Frontières (MSF) revealed that the violence in Darfur was a major cause of mortality among refugees and Chadian returnees crossing into Tissi to escape the violence in Darfur.

According to MSF, "61 percent of the 194 reported deaths were caused by violence, most of them (111 out of 119) by gunshots and linked to specific episodes of violence preceding the two major waves of displacements, one in early February and the other in early April."

Nine out of 10 deaths MSF recorded during its assessment were caused by gunshot wounds. In east Darfur alone, an estimated 305 people had been killed as a result of violent clashes between the Rizeigat and Ma'alia tribes in August alone.

Peacekeepers, too, have not been spared. In July seven peacekeepers with the UN mission there were killed in an ambush—the worst in the five-year history of the UN peacekeeping operations in Sudan—bringing to 13 the number of peacekeepers killed in Darfur since October 2012.

Some 50,000 Darfur refugees have crossed into Chad. The UN Refugee Agency (UNHCR) has described it as the "largest influx of Sudanese refugees into Chad since 2005."

Officials in Darfur have admitted that the violence is now beyond the control of the state.

"[The] state is not in control of the situation nor is it able to disperse the fighting," Abdul Hamid Musa Kasha, governor of east Darfur, told Radio Dabanga.

Who Are the Combatants?

The conflict in Darfur is being waged on many fronts and by different actors. It involves three main rebel groups fighting the government: the SLA (Sudan Liberation Army)-Abdul Wahid faction, the SLA-Minni Minawi faction, and the Justice and Equality Movement (JEM). And while all these rebel groups are fighting under the auspices of the Sudanese Revolutionary Front, they are also divided largely along ethnic lines, with the SLA-Abdul Wahid faction being drawn mainly from the Fur tribe, and the SLA-Minni Minawi and JEM originally being drawn many from the Zaghawa tribe.

Meanwhile, there is inter-tribal violence between the Misseriya and Salamat, and another conflict between the Reizegat and Beni Hussein ethnic groups.

Cutts told IRIN: "This year we have also seen a new wave of localized conflict, including not only the familiar fighting between Arab and non-Arab tribes [e.g. between the Beni Halba and the Gimir; and between the Beni Halba and the Dajo] but also an increase in intra-Arab fighting [e.g. between the Salamat and the Misseriya; and most recently between the Rezeigat and the Maaliya]."

There have been clashes between government forces and militia too. In July there were violent clashes between government forces and Arab militia in the Darfur capital of Nyala, leaving many dead and many more displaced.

What Is Driving the Conflict?

"Underpinning almost all of the conflicts in Darfur are the disputes over land ownership and land use. Indeed, much of what is commonly referred to as "inter-tribal fighting" or fighting over "economic resources" actually relates primarily to disputes over

Ongoing Violence in Darfur, December 2010

Renewed fighting began on December 10, when government forces carried out large-scale attacks on the SLA-controlled area of Khor Abeche and surrounding villages in the Shearia locality of South Darfur. The area is populated largely by ethnic Zaghawa, whom the government accuses of supporting [Minni] Minawi [a rebel leader].

One eyewitness, Adam A., 50, told Human Rights Watch that on December 10 he saw an Antonov airplane flying over the village, followed by 15 military vehicles carrying uniformed soldiers and accompanied by militia members on horse and camel. He said the soldiers went to an SLA [Sudanese Liberation Army, a rebel group] police post in the center of town and encountered one rebel, then proceeded to the market, looting shops and beating civilians with sticks. Among those injured were his wife, who sustained injuries to her head, and many other women, children, and elderly people.

A 30-year-old mother of four gave a similar account: "The soldiers went to the market and started beating people, including women and old men, with sticks and the butts of their guns. I was

land and access to water and grazing for animals," Cutts told IRIN.

The recent clashes in Darfur have mostly been as a result of inter-tribal disputes over grazing land and gold-mining rights.

In January, violence broke out between the Northern Reizegat and Beni Hussein ethnic groups over control of gold mines in the Jebel Amir area of North Darfur State.

"The gold rush in Sudan is further complicating matters. At the beginning of the year there were over 60,000 migrant gold workers in North Darfur alone. In January, disputes over gold mining rights drew two Arab tribes, the Beni Hussein and the Northern Rezeigat, into a conflict that resulted in many deaths

able to take my children and some clothes and flee. All our remaining things were completely burned."

Witnesses told Human Rights Watch that approximately 20 SLA rebels were present in the market at the time of the attack, but that most of the forces had left the area in November [2010] when Minawi's relations with the government began to sour.

The following day, December 11, a convoy of government soldiers again arrived on the outskirts of town, and shot into populated areas with mounted machine guns. During this attack, they killed two civilians and injured more than a dozen others. Witnesses said the army was accompanied by Popular Defense Forces, an auxiliary force that has absorbed many of the so-called "Janjaweed" militia.

The attacks and clashes also caused massive damage to civilian property, with more than 60 homes reported burned in Khor Abeche, including that of the *umda*, or community leader. Government and rebel forces again clashed on December 17 and 18, causing more property destruction and displacement of the population.

"Darfur in the Shadows: The Sudanese Government's Ongoing Attacks on Civilians and Human Rights," Human Rights Watch, June 6, 2011, pp. 11–12.

and the displacement of over 100,000 people. And this was not the first violent incident related to gold mining in Darfur," said Cutts.

Analysts fear the competition for other resources such as gum Arabic might lead to future violent inter-communal conflicts.

In July, Human Security Baseline Assessment for Sudan (HBAS), part of the Small Arms Survey, a project of the Graduate Institute of International and Development Studies, noted: "New conflict trends have emerged in 2013. The most prominent of these, resource-based conflict in the Jebel Amir area of North Darfur over control of artisanal gold mining and trade, began in January 2013. . . .

"Other resources have also generated inter-communal violence: in South Darfur, the Gimir and Bani Halba have clashed over the harvesting of gum Arabic," it added.

What Are the Challenges Facing Aid Agencies?

The deteriorating security situation has meant many aid agencies are unable to keep their staff on the ground in Darfur. Some have had their field offices looted.

In July an international NGO was robbed of an estimated US$40,000 when armed men entered their office in Central Darfur's capital, Zalingei. In the same month, armed men stopped two buses and five trucks near Thur in Nertiti Locality while on their way from Zalingei to Nyala in South Darfur. The drivers and passengers were robbed of all personal items; one passenger was shot and injured while resisting the attack.

In May, two vehicles rented by an international NGO and carrying seven staff were carjacked in Wadi Salih Locality.

Earlier in February, the rented vehicle of another international NGO was ambushed north of Zalingei. Staff were robbed of all personal possessions.

"Commercial transporters are currently unwilling to transport relief supplies from El Geneina (West Darfur) and Zalingei to areas in the southern corridor localities—mainly Mukjar, Um Dukhun and Bindisi—due to security concerns," OCHA said in its July bulletin.

Sudanese analyst Eric Reeves, a professor at the Smith College (USA), said in a recent analysis that "over the past year and more . . . violence has called into serious question the viability of any substantial ongoing relief efforts in the region. Virtually no international (expatriate) staff remain in Darfur, certainly not in the field or in remote locations—either for critical assessment work or to provide oversight for aid distribution. And as the recent killing of two workers for World Vision in their Nyala compound makes clear, there is no place of real safety in Darfur."

OCHA's Cutts told IRIN that while aid agencies have access to most of those in need in Darfur, "the continued insecurity and fighting and government restrictions on movement" had clearly affected aid agencies' ability to operate.

"This has a direct impact on the ability of humanitarian actors to assess humanitarian needs and to ensure that people in need receive the assistance they require, particularly in areas of ongoing conflict," he added.

In its 2013 World Report, Human Rights Watch said the Sudanese regime "continued to deny peacekeepers from the United Nations African Union Mission in Darfur (UNAMID) access to much of Darfur" and that "lawlessness and insecurity hampered the work of the peacekeepers and aid groups. Armed gunmen attacked and killed peacekeepers, including four Nigerians in October, abducted UNAMID and humanitarian staff and carjacked dozens of vehicles."

According to Smith College's Reeves, "opportunistic banditry has grown steadily and become a deeply debilitating threat to humanitarian operations. Fighting among Arab tribal groups has been a constant for a number of years, and has contributed steadily to instability and violence in Darfur."

The Sudanese government too stands accused: "Khartoum has deliberately crippled UNAMID as an effective force for civilian and humanitarian protection. Opposed from the beginning by the regime, the mission cannot begin to fulfil its UN Security Council civilian protection mandate, and indeed operates only insofar as Khartoum's security forces permit," Reeves noted.

What Is the Status of the Peace Process?

Numerous peace processes to end the conflict between the government of Sudan and the various armed groups operating in Darfur have not borne much fruit. These include one in Abuja in 2006, and another in 2007 in the Libyan capital, Tripoli. The latest such initiative was in Doha.

Signed between the Sudanese government and armed groups, they have generally been dogged by a lack of legitimacy and deemed not inclusive enough.

"The second challenge concerns poor implementation of the DDPD [Doha Document for Peace in Darfur] and a lack of inclusivity. Promised funds from both the government of Sudan and donors have been slow to arrive, which has further delayed the activities of the Darfur Regional Authority (DRA), established in December 2011 as the lead actor for the implementation of the agreement," said the HBAS report.

"The third challenge to the formal peace process is the significant deterioration in security across Darfur in 2013, as local peace mechanisms struggle to contain inter-communal violence, exacerbated by government actions."

Locally, state officials say they are mulling the idea of bringing together leaders of the warring tribes to cease hostilities and bring the conflict to an end.

CHAPTER 2

Controversies Surrounding Mass Atrocities in Darfur

Chapter Exercises

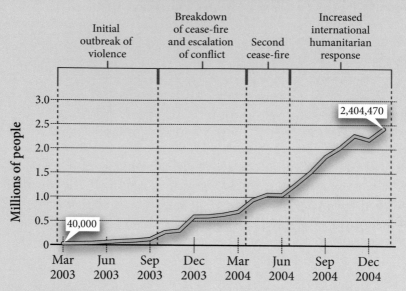

ESTIMATE OF POPULATION AFFECTED BY THE CONFLICT IN DARFUR

Data source: United Nations.

Source: Bureau of Intelligence and Research Fact Sheet, "Sudan: Death Toll in Darfur," US Department of State, March 25, 2005. http://2001-2009.state.gov/s/inr/rls/fs/2005 /45105.htm.

1. Analyze the Chart

Question 1: How many people were estimated to be affected by the conflict in Darfur shortly after it started in 2003? What was the estimated amount when the April 2004 cease-fire was declared? What was the estimated amount near the end of 2004?

Question 2: What effect did the cease-fires have on the number of people displaced by the conflict? Did the number increase more or less rapidly after April 2004? What intervention or event might have had an opposite result?

Question 3: Does the data in the chart support or undermine the argument for the need for an international humanitarian response in Darfur? Explain.

2. Writing Prompt

Write an editorial passionately arguing either that Darfur is a genocide or that it is not a genocide. Use evidence and facts from the readings in this chapter to support your argument.

3. Group Activity

Form two groups for a debate. One group will adopt the position that the crisis in Darfur was caused by climate change and competition for natural resources. The other group will adopt the position that the crisis in Darfur was caused by long-standing distrust and animosity between ethnic groups.

Darfur Is a Genocide

Salih Booker and Ann-Louise Colgan

Salih Booker is executive director and Ann-Louise Colgan is assistant director for policy analysis and communications at the advocacy group Africa Action. In the following viewpoint, they argue that the violence in Darfur in 2003–2004 constitutes genocide, and the United States and the United Nations should immediately recognize it as such. The authors suggest that commercial oil interests and diplomatic concerns about the fragility of the peace deal between North and South Sudan has kept the international community from declaring Darfur a genocide. However, the authors conclude that the international community has a moral obligation to intervene.

Ten years after Rwanda [the systematic massacre of the minority Tutsi ethnic group by the majority Hutu ethnic group in 1994], a genocide is unfolding again while the world watches and refuses to say its name. The failure of the United States and the international community to act in Rwanda a decade ago cost 800,000 lives. Now, up to 1 million people face a similar fate in Darfur, western Sudan, as a result of an ongoing government

Salih Booker, "Genocide in Darfur." Reprinted with permission from the July 12, 2004, issue of *The Nation*. For subscription information, call 1-800-333-8536. Portions of each week's *Nation* magazine can be accessed at http://thenation.com. Copyright © 2004 The Nation.

REPORTS OF VIOLENCE BY DARFUR REFUGEES

Percent witnessing or experiencing the following:

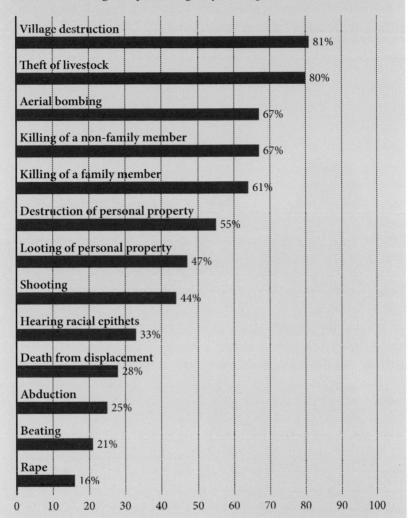

Village destruction — 81%

Theft of livestock — 80%

Aerial bombing — 67%

Killing of a non-family member — 67%

Killing of a family member — 61%

Destruction of personal property — 55%

Looting of personal property — 47%

Shooting — 44%

Hearing racial epithets — 33%

Death from displacement — 28%

Abduction — 25%

Beating — 21%

Rape — 16%

| 0 | 10 | 20 | 30 | 40 | 50 | 60 | 70 | 80 | 90 | 100 |

Note: Reported atrocities were included in the data set only if the respondent directly witnessed the event. A respondent was considered to have "directly witnessed" an atrocity if she or he was an eyewitness to the event, visually confirmed the death of victims, or, in cases of rape, was directly told about the atrocity by the victim. Hearsay accounts were excluded from the data set.

Source: US Department of State, "Documenting Atrocities in Darfur," State Publication 11182, September 2004. http://2001-2009.state.gov/g/drl/rls/36028.htm.

campaign to destroy a portion of its population. What is happening in Darfur is genocide, and must be called that. The term "genocide" not only captures the fundamental characteristics of the Khartoum government's intent and actions, it also invokes clear international obligations.

Yet, as horrifying reports continue to emerge, and as a humanitarian emergency grows, there is no indication that the United States or the United Nations is prepared to intervene—despite promises of "never again" and explicit obligations under the 1948

Convention on Genocide. For more than a year, the Khartoum government has systematically obstructed access to Darfur and blocked international efforts to establish a relief program. More recently, it has failed to honor the cease-fire it signed in April [2004]. As a result, Darfur now faces the worst humanitarian crisis in the world, with 30,000 people already killed and more than a million internally displaced. International aid agencies

A Sudanese refugee walks past the site of four mass graves, each raised mound marked by a white sack, in the Kalma refugee camp in 2008. © AP Photo/Sarah El Deeb.

say that even if humanitarian relief arrives now, 350,000 people may still die.

Geographic, Religious, Racial, and Ethnic Conflicts

Sudan, geographically Africa's largest country, has experienced civil war with only a ten-year pause since independence in 1956. More than 2 million people have been killed and twice that many displaced in the long-running war between successive governments of the north and peoples of the south. Recent progress toward peace has brought hope that this troubled history will finally come to a close, but the growing crisis in Darfur, which began last year, casts a dark shadow. In Darfur, the Sudanese government is destroying African Muslim communities because some among them have challenged Khartoum's authoritarian rule. As in the conflict between north and south, in Darfur ethnic and racial identities have also been part of the conflict. But at its heart is a repressive minority Arab-centric regime in Khartoum that rules by force, cannot even claim to represent a majority of northerners and has relied on religious fundamentalism to maintain its power.

The International Obligation to Intervene

Ironically, the international community's unwillingness to intervene results—at least in part—from concern that a fragile peace deal between north and south will be jeopardized. Across several administrations, the United States has been involved in promoting peace in Sudan, and the Bush Administration is eager to claim credit for its diplomatic efforts. But as long as the Sudanese government is waging a genocidal war in Darfur, the United States cannot pretend that a meaningful peace deal can be achieved. The Administration had hoped that such an agreement would allow it to lift sanctions on Sudan. This, in turn, would permit US oil companies to pursue a share of the country's recently developed oil wealth. Such interests, however, cannot be allowed to compromise a larger moral obligation.

As parties to the Genocide Convention, all permanent members of the UN Security Council, including the United States and more than 130 countries worldwide, are bound to prevent and punish genocide. The convention names genocide as a crime in international law, describing it as the commission of acts with "intent to destroy, in whole or in part, a national, ethnical, racial or religious group."

The Security Council continues to hesitate on Darfur, largely because of the economic and diplomatic interests of its permanent members, who don't wish to antagonize Khartoum. Whether the UN can be spurred to action will depend largely on the United States, and Washington has an obligation to act. One reason is its treaty obligations under the Genocide Convention. Another is its involvement in Sudan's peace process, supported by an eclectic domestic constituency, including groups ranging from the evangelical right to the Congressional Black Caucus. A third is the unique US intelligence capacity to track militia activity in Darfur as well as the movements of the displaced. Finally, it has 1,800 troops in nearby Djibouti, some of whom could be mobilized quickly to lead a multinational force to secure the region, to facilitate humanitarian assistance and to enforce the cease-fire until a UN peacekeeping force can be assembled.

When George W. Bush hosted the G-8 summit in June [2004], the leaders of the world's richest and most powerful countries merely urged the government of Sudan to disarm the militias. Were this tragedy unfolding in Europe, their summit would have focused on little other than intervention. Unless there is an immediate military intervention in Darfur, up to a million people could die this year. We should have learned from Rwanda that to stop genocide, Washington must first say the word.

Darfur Is Not a Genocide

Jonathan Steele

Jonathan Steele is a foreign correspondent for The Guardian. *In the following viewpoint, he argues that the violence in Darfur is more accurately characterized as a civil war, not a genocide. He also says that both sides have committed atrocities, and it is the rebels—not the government—who have refused peace deals. He concludes that the international community has been right to limit the intervention of peacekeeping forces and suggests that a modest increase in resources for these forces is probably the best policy going forward.*

An air of unreality, if not cant, surrounds the latest upsurge of calls for UN troops to go into Sudan's western region of Darfur. The actor George Clooney takes to the stage at the UN security council, pleading for action. [British Prime Minister] Tony Blair seizes on the issue to write letters to fellow EU leaders. In cities around the world protesters hold a "global day for Darfur" to warn of looming genocide. Is it really possible that western governments, in spite of being burned by their interventions in Iraq and Afghanistan, would use force against another Muslim state?

Groups in the west have long campaigned to have the government in Khartoum [Sudan] replaced. In the US the Christian right and some of Israel's friends portray it as an Islamic fundamentalist regime. Human rights activists raise the issue of slavery to suggest that Arab raiders, supported by the government, are routinely abducting Africans from the south to use as human chattel. The [US president Bill] Clinton administration listed Sudan as a terrorist-supporting state because [al Qaeda terrorist group leader] Osama bin Laden once lived there.

Against this background it was always going to be hard to expect fair reporting when civil war broke out in Darfur three years ago [as of 2006]. The complex grievances that set farmers against nomads was covered with a simplistic template of Arab versus African, even though the region was crisscrossed with tribal and local rivalries that put some villages on the government's side and others against it.

A Brutal Civil War—Not Ethnic Cleansing

It is true that the government, as often happens in asymmetrical war, overreacted in its use of force when rebels attacked. The so-called janjaweed militias that Khartoum organised and armed did not distinguish between civilians and guerrilla fighters. They burned huts, raped women and put tens of thousands of civilians to flight, forcing them across the border into Chad or into camps inside Darfur. But the rebels also committed atrocities, a fact that was rarely reported since it upset the black-and-white moral image that many editors preferred.

In most wars, governments spin and the media (at least sometimes) seek the truth. Darfur reversed the trend: the media spun while governments were more sophisticated. In spite of efforts to describe the killing in Darfur as genocide, neither the UN nor the EU went along with this description. It was not because of moral myopia, but because they understood the difference between a brutal civil war and a deliberate policy of ethnic cleansing. Darfur is not Rwanda. Only the US accepted the genocide

description, though this seemed a concession to domestic lob-
bies rather than a matter of conviction. Washington never followed through with the forcible intervention in Darfur that international law requires once a finding of genocide is made.

Missteps by All Sides Prevent Peace

Instead, it supported other western governments in encouraging
the African Union (AU) to broker peace talks between Khartoum
and the rebels. These culminated in May [2006] in an agreement
that requires the janjaweed to disarm before the rebels do. It also
gives Darfur's rebel leaders powers to run the region on their
own. Alas, two rebel groups refused to sign. Any fair account of
this summer's relapse into war would therefore put most blame
on the rebels, whose field commanders recently split into rival
groups while their political leaders squabbled in their safe ha-
vens in the Eritrean capital, Asmara.

They may have legitimate reasons for arguing that the peace
deal did not give enough. Some of the displaced say Khartoum
should have to pay families compensation. Others say the peace
deal has no enforcement measures and fails to protect people
who want to go back to rebuild their villages. But the answer is
to conduct more talks, not resume the war. African and western diplomats are trying to get the rebels to think again, but
find themselves frustrated by the rebels' feuds. Blair's letter on
Darfur was careful to call for pressure on the rebels as well as
Khartoum, even though most of the media chose to see it as
one-dimensional.

Lack of Support for the Peacekeeping Forces

Putting international peace monitors into Darfur to protect the
displaced in their camps was vital. Two years ago the Khartoum
government accepted this. It allowed the AU to deploy 7,000
troops. But, short of money, helicopters, and other equipment,
the AU went along with western governments earlier this year in
asking the UN to take over. This is where the debate is now. No

Sudan Liberation Army (SLA) fighters ride in a truck in 2004 in Thabit, North Darfur. Some argue that both sides of the conflict have committed atrocities, making it a civil war and not a genocide. © Jacob Silberberg/Getty Images.

one expects that western troops are going to move into Sudan. It has taken weeks to bolster the UN force in Lebanon, while in Afghanistan most Nato members have held back from sending troops into a failing war. In practice, a UN force would be nothing more than the existing AU one with reinforcements, perhaps from India and Bangladesh.

So, behind all the clamour for UN intervention, what is really being discussed is a change in badges. Having AU troops to handle an African problem has symbolic, cultural and political value. But African governments are overstretched, whereas the UN has an established system of subsidising troop-supplying governments. Ironically, given the demands in the US for firm action, it was Congress that recently refused to fund [President George W.] Bush's request for help to the AU.

What of the effort to indict Sudanese leaders for committing atrocities before an international court? Fear of arrest is said to be one reason why Sudan's president Omar al-Bashir has blocked UN troops. Even if a UN force were still 90% African, he might think it could include a western-piloted snatch squad tasked to capture him or his Darfurian lieutenants. If that were the case, the security council resolution that recently called on Khartoum to accept a UN force carefully avoided any reference to international trials. So did an EU statement last week.

Hope for a Compromise

In practice, then, there is a good chance that this week's negotiations at the UN will produce a compromise—neither the existing African Union force nor a new UN one, but a hybrid. It could be an AU force with African leadership but under a UN mandate and answerable to the security council. Its contingents might include non-Africans but its mandate would be little different from the current one. After the huffing and puffing of the past few days, this would be a sensible outcome.

Suspicions remain on all sides. Khartoum feels betrayed by the US. After making a peace deal in the south that rules out sharia [that is, Islamic] law and provides for a referendum on secession, it expected US sanctions would be lifted. It felt it had shown it was not fundamentalist or even Islamist since its new government of national unity includes southern Christians and other non-Muslims. As for terrorism, Washington has produced no evidence for a decade.

Meanwhile, many of Khartoum's critics suspect the government has not abandoned its indiscriminate bombing raids and excessive use of force against rebel villages. No foreign peacekeepers, whether AU or UN, can monitor all the vast terrain of Darfur. Sudan's government must discipline its own commanders. That said, the compromise of an expanded AU force, whether labelled UN or not, is still the best option. The "something must be done" brigade will be upset, but sending foreign troops into Sudan without Khartoum's consent would be nothing short of disaster.

The Arrest Warrant for the Sudanese President Strengthened International Justice

Andrew G. Reiter

Andrew G. Reiter is a professor of politics at Mount Holyoke College in South Hadley, Massachusetts. In the following viewpoint, he reports that the president of Sudan, Omar al-Bashir, was forced to cancel a trip to the United Nations in 2013 for fear of arrest on a warrant for war crimes from the International Criminal Court. Reiter says that this episode strengthens international justice efforts and shows that heads of state can no longer expect blanket immunity from arrest for crimes against humanity.

In 2009, the International Criminal Court [ICC] issued an arrest warrant for Sudan's Omar al-Bashir on charges of crimes against humanity and war crimes committed in Darfur and expanded those charges to include genocide in 2010. Yet al-Bashir recently claimed immunity as a head of state and requested a visa from the United States to travel freely to New York to participate in the UN General Assembly and return safely to the comfort of his palace in Khartoum. In a *Marbury v. Madison* [the 1803 court case which established the power of the US judicial branch] moment for the ICC, the battle between immunity and the reach of

Surrounded by security, Sudanese president Omar al-Bashir (center) gestures to his supporters during a 2008 tour of El Fasher in North Darfur. He is estimated to be responsible for the deaths of 2.5 million people in Sudan. © Khaled Desouki/AFP/Getty Images.

international criminal law was in the hands of the US. A strong position by the US that it could not guarantee al-Bashir would not be arrested forced him to cancel his trip; a move that significantly advances international justice and helps the ICC come of age.

In referring the initial case to the ICC, the UN Security Council urged all states to cooperate fully with the court; and in issuing the arrest warrant, the Court formally requested cooperation in obtaining al-Bashir's arrest to all state parties and

Omar al-Bashir

Omar al-Bashir, the president of Sudan, took power in a 1989 coup with the goal of replacing feuding political parties with Islamic law. But history will almost certainly remember him for his roles in two murderous civil wars. Bashir led his nation through 15 years of bloody civil war between the central government and rebels in southern Sudan. A peace agreement in 2005 ended that conflict. But starting in 2003, Bashir responded to a new rebellion in Sudan's western region of Darfur with such vicious force, many world leaders called it genocide.

Writing in *Time* in 2007, humanitarian activists Don Cheadle and John Prendergast called Bashir one of the world's five worst dictators since World War II. They charged that his war strategies resulted in the deaths of 2.5 million people in Darfur and southern Sudan and the destruction of 1,500 villages, leaving seven million people homeless. According to *New York Times* journalists Marlise Simons, Lydia Polgreen, and Jeffrey Gettleman, a war-crimes prosecutor agreed. In 2008, he asked judges in the International Criminal Court to indict Bashir on charges of genocide and crimes against humanity.

Omar Hassan Ahmed Bashir was born in January of 1944 to a farming couple in a village in the Nile Valley in northern Sudan. He joined the military at age 16 and graduated from Sudan's military academy in 1966. He fought alongside Egyptian forces in the 1973

UN Security Council members. Yet most states have simply ignored the warrant, treating him like any other foreign dignitary. He has traveled to a number of neighboring countries in Africa, attended several regional summits, and made very visible trips to Egypt and China.

The key issue has been the concept of immunity in customary international law, which gives heads of state protection from criminal prosecutions or arrests in other states, and leaders have long enjoyed its benefits and feel it is vital to the peaceful con-

war with Israel and was Sudan's military liaison to the United Arab Emirates from 1975 to 1979, a garrison commander from 1979 to 1981, and head of the armored parachute brigade in Khartoum from 1981 to 1987.

Bashir served a tour of duty in the fight against rebels in the southern part of the country. Since gaining its independence in 1956, Sudan, Africa's largest country, has been ruled by the Arabs in northern Sudan, around Khartoum, the capital, while Christian and animist tribes in southern Sudan have resisted Arab rule. The conflict grew into an open civil war in 1983, after the central government instituted rule by Islamic sharia law. An uprising led to the suspension of sharia law in 1986, but the civil war continued.

On June 30, 1989, Bashir seized power in Sudan, leading a military coup that overthrew Prime Minister Sadiq al-Mahdi and his democratically elected government. In a televised address, Bashir declared he had mounted the coup "to save the country from rotten political parties," according to the BBC News. He quickly banned political parties and dissolved the country's parliament. To run the country, he set up the 15-member Revolutionary Command Council for National Salvation, which he chaired. Bashir also announced he was abandoning a peace agreement in southern Sudan. In April of 1990, the regime executed 31 army and police officers, allegedly for plotting a coup, though journalists and diplomats reported that was a pretext for eliminating people the regime did not trust.

"Omar al-Bashir," Newsmakers, vol. 2. Detroit: Gale, 2009.

tinuation of diplomacy worldwide. The International Court of Justice has gone as far as ruling that immunity is necessary for governments to be able to function effectively.

No Head-of-State Immunity for Serious International Crimes

And al-Bashir's most recent attempt to visit the UN was not a normal case of immunity. The UN Charter, the Convention on the Privileges and Immunities of the United Nations, and the UN

Headquarters Agreement all guarantee that representatives of states be allowed to attend UN meetings, and the US, as the host country, is obligated to not impose any impediments to travel. In the past, the UN has taken a firm stand in favor of the immunity that protects its delegations: disallowing attempts to block the attendance of representatives from Israel and South Africa, and moving a 1988 meeting to Geneva in response to the US denying a visa for Yassar Arafat.

Immunity, however, has been slowly eroding for serious international crimes, evidenced most dramatically by the charges brought against Charles Taylor by the Special Court for Sierra Leone while he was still president of Liberia. And the ICC has made it clear that it does not view immunity as a defense in its cases, ruling firmly that it does not apply to international crimes, and arguing that one of the "core goals" of the Court is to end immunity.

The lack of state cooperation on al-Bashir has caused the Court to become more assertive. In July [2013], it demanded that Nigeria arrest al-Bashir and surrender him to the court, forcing him to leave an African Union summit early. In response to this recent attempt to attend the UN, the Court's judges took the dramatic step of releasing a statement requesting the US government arrest al-Bashir if he enters US territory.

The United States' Strategic Decision

The US is not a party to the Rome Statue, and thus not required to honor the ICC arrest warrant. Moreover, the immunity protections deeply embedded in how the UN operates legally allow heads of state to attend, likely resulting in significant diplomatic ramifications if the US were to block or arrest al-Bashir. Yet the UN Security Council played a prominent role in referring the al-Bashir case to the ICC, and the Obama administration has worked openly to strengthen the US's relationship with the Court, even using it during the crisis in Libya in 2011 [a civil war in which the US intervened].

The US and the ICC thus found themselves at a critical juncture, and the US responded by pressuring al-Bashir to stay home. The move serves to strengthen the diplomatic isolation that an ICC arrest warrant brings, weakens the international concept of immunity in cases of gross human rights violations, and strengthens the power of the ICC. The end result is a dramatic step forward for international justice.

The Arrest Warrant for the Sudanese President Was Seriously Flawed

Antonio Cassese

Antonio Cassese, the first president of the International Criminal Tribunal for the Former Yugoslavia, and later the chairperson of the UN International Commission of Inquiry on Darfur, teaches law at the University of Florence in Italy. In the following viewpoint, he argues that the arrest warrant for Sudanese president Omar al-Bashir was poorly handled. He says that the warrant failed to include other important people responsible for the genocide. Furthermore, he argues that the indictment should have been sealed so that Bashir wouldn't have been warned, and it should have included crimes other than genocide. He concluded that the warrant might lead Bashir to interfere with humanitarian aid and could destabilize Sudan and cause more violence.

Those who follow events in Darfur closely know very well that Sudan's President Omar Hassan al-Bashir leads a group of political and military leaders responsible for the serious and large-scale crimes against Sudanese citizens that the country's military forces, with the assistance of paramilitary groups and militias, commit every day in the region. These citizens are guilty only of belonging to the three tribes (Fur, Masalit, and Zaghawa) that spawned the rebels who took up arms against the government a few years ago.

Any step designed to hold Sudan's leaders accountable for their crimes is therefore most welcome. Nevertheless, the decision of Luis Moreno-Ocampo, the Prosecutor of the International Criminal Court, to request an arrest warrant against al-Bashir is puzzling, for three reasons.

Three Flaws of the Arrest Warrant

First, if Moreno-Ocampo intended to pursue the goal of having al-Bashir arrested, he might have issued a sealed request and asked the ICC's judges to issue a sealed arrest warrant, to be made public only once al-Bashir traveled abroad. The Court's jurisdiction over the crimes in Darfur has been established pursuant to a binding decision of the United Nations Security Council, which means that even states that are not parties to the ICC statute must execute the Court's orders and warrants. Having instead made the request for a warrant public, al-Bashir—assuming the judges uphold the request—can simply refrain from traveling abroad and thus avoid arrest.

Second, Moreno-Ocampo has inexplicably decided to indict only Sudan's president and not also the other members of the political and military leadership that together with him have planned, ordered, and organized the massive crimes in Darfur. If Hitler had been alive in October 1945, the 21 indictees who were in fact tried at Nuremberg [a war crimes trial for perpetrators of the Holocaust] would not have been let off the hook.

Finally, one fails to understand why Moreno-Ocampo has aimed so high and accused al-Bashir of the "crime of crimes," genocide, instead of filing charges that are more appropriate and easier to prosecute, such as war crimes (bombing of civilians) and crimes against humanity (extermination, forcible transfer of people, massive murders, rape, etc.). True, genocide has become a magic word, and people think that its mere evocation triggers the strong outrage of the world community and perforce sets in motion UN intervention. But this is not so.

The Challenge of Proving Genocide

Moreover, strict conditions must be met to prove genocide. In particular, the victims must form an ethnic, religious, racial, or national group, and the perpetrator must entertain "genocidal intent," namely the will to destroy the group as such, in whole or in part. For example, one kills ten Kurds not because they are obnoxious or because the perpetrator has strong feelings against each of them taken individually, but only because they are Kurds; by killing those ten persons he intends to contribute to the destruction of the group as such.

In the case of Darfur, according to Moreno-Ocampo, each of the three tribes does constitute an ethnic group; although they speak the same language as the majority (Arabic) and embrace the same religion (Islam) and their skin is the same color, they constitute distinct ethnic groups because each tribe also speaks a dialect and lives in a particular area. Under this standard, the inhabitants of many European regions—for example, Sicilians, who, in addition to the official language, also speak a dialect and live in a particular area—should be regarded as distinct "ethnic groups."

Furthermore, Moreno-Ocampo has inferred al-Bashir's genocidal intent from a set of facts and conduct that in his view amount to a clear indication of such intent. However, according to the international case law, one can prove by inference a defendant's state of mind only if the inference is the only reasonable one that can be drawn based on the evidence. In the case of Darfur, it would seem more reasonable to infer from the evidence the intent to commit crimes against humanity (extermination, etc.), rather than the intent to annihilate ethnic groups in whole or in part.

The Likelihood of Unintended Consequences

The arrest warrant, assuming that the ICC issues it, seems unlikely to produce the extra-judicial effects—the political and moral delegitimization of the accused—that sometimes follow. This happened in the case of former Bosnian Serb leader Radovan Karadzic, who, although never arrested, has been removed both from power and the international arena as a result of his indictment in 1995.

Instead, Moreno-Ocampo's request may have negative political repercussions by creating much disarray in international relations. It may harden the Sudanese government's position, endanger the survival of the peace-keeping forces in Darfur, and even induce al-Bashir to take revenge by stopping or making even more difficult the flow of international humanitarian assistance to the two million displaced persons in Darfur. On top of that, Moreno-Ocampo's request might further alienate the Great Powers (China, Russia, and the United States) that are currently hostile to the ICC.

The Conflict in Darfur Is Rooted in Longstanding Ethnic and Religious Differences

Usman A. Tar

Usman A. Tar is the managing editor of Information, Society, and Justice, *a journal based at London Metropolitan University, and the author of* The Politics of Neoliberal Democracy in Africa. *In the following viewpoint, he argues that Sudan has long been extremely heterogeneous both ethnically and religiously. These divisions have laid the groundwork for almost ceaseless violence since the country gained independence. The divisions formed the basis for conflicts between northern Muslim Sudan and the non-Muslim southern region, he says, but they have also fueled inter-Muslim fighting between Arab and other ethnicities in Darfur.*

Greater Darfur, a territory roughly the size of France or Texas and with an estimated population of about four to five million people, is Sudan's largest region in terms of landmass and population. Yet it is one of the least developed regions in the country with a long history of ethnic and racial strife. Located in the north-western region of the country, the region shares Sudan's international borders with the Republic of Chad to the west, Libya to the northwest and Central Africa Republic to the southwest. In the context of the on-going insurgency and its drastic aftermaths, however, the border region between Chad and Sudan provides flashpoint of the crisis. There is a long history of migration and commerce across the border and today people traverse both sides of the political divide for economic activities. Indeed, during the colonial era, Darfur served as one of the two main axes of Sudan's international trade.

The ecology of the area ranging from desert in the north, fertile belt in the Jabel Marra region to mixed vegetation of the southern zone provides a massive resource base for agriculture resulting in conflict between sedentary farmers and itinerary nomads. In the past, such clashes have occurred between mainly Fur, Masalit and other 'African' farming communities [and] pastoralist 'Arab' tribes, particularly those from Beni Hussein from Kabkabiya region (North Darfur) and Beni Halba (South Darfur). Following administrative divisions in 1994, Darfur has been divided into three provinces: North, South and West. West Darfur comprises mainly of the Fur and Masalit, albeit with a panoramic mixture of other ethnic groups. The pattern of farmers-pastoralists clashes cut across the three administrative divisions of Darfur but intensifies as a result of annual migration by pastoralists seeking greener pasture for their livestock.

The Traditional Approach to Conflict Resolution

In the past, clashes between cattle and camel rearing Arab tribes and sedentary African farming communities were often resolved through age hallowed means of conflict resolution reinforced by Anglo-Egyptian legal heritages. Acting as third party mediators, community leaders and tribal chiefs—Sheikh Kabilah—often serve as veritable tools for conflict management. These traditional mediation mechanisms often prove fruitful resulting in compensations for lost crops, establishing the time and pattern of seasonal migration, as well as setting buffer zones for grazing. Nevertheless, they also fail to resolve the conflict or even degenerate into further strife. For instance in January 1999, Arab and Masalit tribal heads gathered to restore normalcy following a standoff between farmers and pastoralists over the latter's grazing on former's cultivated farmland. The arbitration collapsed when angry Masalit farmers shot at the tribal heads killing an Arab chief. Political interference, undue influence and biased top-level conspiracies did nothing more than to further add insult to the injury:

> The Sudanese government claimed that the Masalit were fifth column of the Sudan's People Liberation Army . . . and sealed off Dar Masalit. Reportedly the Arab militias then killed more than 1,000 Masalit. The government set up special courts to try leaders of the clashes, sentencing fourteen people to death, and sponsored a tribal reconciliation conference [which] concluded that 292 Masalit and seven Arabs were dead; 2,673 houses burned down; and large numbers of livestock looted, with Masalit suffering most. The Arabs refused [to] pay compensation. About 29,500 fearful Masalit refugees remained in Chad, where the Arab militia reportedly came to kill eighty Masalit refugees in mid-1999.

From the foregoing statement, an indicator of the partisan role of the state is its indictment of the Masalit, thus giving tacit approval for Arab militia to vent their anger, before setting up judicial process to try offenders perhaps in terms convenient to the government. Thus, though the conflict over resources in Darfur is age-long, over the past two decades or so, it has been intensified by several political, security and socio-economic factors: . . . a combination of extended periods of drought; competition for dwindling resources; lack of good governance and democracy; and easy availability of guns have made local clashes increasingly bloody and politicised.

Natural and Man-Made Tragedies

Among the factors mentioned above, two of them—one natural, the other manmade—devastatingly changed the course of the

A Sudanese farmer transports straw in Western Darfur in 2007. Conflicts over land between farmers and nomad herders is cited as a basis for the Darfur conflict. © Peter Steffen Deutsche Presse-Agentur/Newscom.

conflict in the late 1980s. The first was the [drought] and famine that struck Darfur in 1984–1985 and left many Arab pastoralists with heavy [loss] of their livestock. As a result, they resorted to raiding the stock of others who were less hit by the catastrophe. Victims who resist or track back the footprint of raiders had to face battle with the raiding gangs leading to loss of human lives and wealth. In addition to raiding, the [drought] also led pastoralists who were left with few malnourished herds to find solace by grazing on farmlands and barns of settled African farmers provoking their anger in the process. The farmers' retaliation to such acts often resulted in violent clashes between farmers and frustrated pastoralists. The second factor which emerged almost at the same period as the [drought] of the late 1980s, was the introduction of small arms into farming and pastoralists communities. While in the distant past, the kinds of arms available

Local Conflicts in Darfur

Regarding Darfur, there is hardly a complex political emergency in the world where so much is known about local political dynamics, the links to external actors and factors, and the core issues related to livelihoods, land, and access to resources. While Darfur's rebels used economic inequality and neglect as a justification for their rebellion, the engine of that insurrection was to a large extent local strife, some but not all instigated by Khartoum. Yet the low-energy mediation led by the AU [African Union], the UN, and other international actors largely failed to move beyond macropolitical cleavages despite rhetoric to the contrary ("Darfur-Darfur dialogue"). One result was that rebel groups without constituencies were invited to join peace talks, thereby contributing to a "ceaseless carousel of fighting and talking". Another consequence was that the civilian population, including most Arab groups and constituencies (frequently demonized as "Janjaweed"), was sidelined from the peace processes.

Abdel Ghaffar M. Ahmed and Gunnar M. Sørbø, eds., "Introduction: Sudan's Durable Disorder," Sudan Divided: Continuing Conflict in a Contested State. New York: Palgrave Macmillan, 2013, pp. 17–18.

to farmers and pastoralist were traditional dane guns, swords, machetes, bows and arrows, the introduction of small arms tragically transformed the violent means of fighting available to rival communities and tribes. By January 1988 it was reported that "there were at least 50,000 automatic weapons in Darfur—one for every sixteen adult men." The proliferation of small arms became worse after the government of Sadiq Al-Mahdi (1986–89) introduced a policy of arming Muraheleen militia in Darfur and Kordofan regions. The proliferation of automatic weapons, fuelled by governmental influence in such an 'unstable state' as Sudan, fits into what [military and defense analysts Rachel] Stohl and [Dan] Smith term 'a deadly combination' by which they mean the lethal configuration of state instability and unfettered proliferation of small arms coupled up with all their associated security risks. Successive regimes in Sudan have continued to abuse the volatile situation by allowing 'loyal' and favoured groups to possess arms as a means of 'defending themselves'.

Allegation of biased and counter-productive interference by successive Sudanese governments not only fermented the conflict in Darfur, but also further politicised ethnic and racial tension among Darfurians of African and Arab identities, especially on such tangential but sensitive macro-political issues as representation and local governance. For a long time, Arabs have shown resentment over their insufficient representation in local governments which, they complain, were dominated mainly by Fur and Masalit. They agitated for a fairer representation by forging pan-Arabic political platforms and interest groups. In 1986, they formed the Arab Alliance, a movement aimed at regaining control of Darfur and stamping Arab influence in the region. This development culminated in allegations by African Darfurians [of the] government's favouring of Arabs on policy making and executions, even if such policies are detrimental to fragile peace and security of the region. Instances of policy biases include appointment of 'Arabs' into sensitive and high-powered posts; the arming of Muraheleen militia, giving them legal protection to commit violence as well as favouritism of Arabs in the dispensation of justice especially over land matters and communal crises. This resulted in breeding feelings of domination and distrust from Fur, Masalit and Zaghawa political leaders, fears that were later proved in 1994 following the President Omar El-Bashir's administrative reforms in Darfur which gave Arab leaders new positions of power. This policy shift was seen as a deliberate and systematic strategy aimed at reversing power imbalances in favour of Arabs and simultaneously undermining the power of 'Africans'.

Resource Conflict Becomes Ethnic Conflict

It was against the backdrop of the foregoing factors and incidences that by 1998/99, the pattern of clashes in Darfur took a tangible shape, in a manner that was not necessarily so in the past: protracted clash between 'African' Fur, Masalit and Zaghawa on the one hand and 'Arabs' on the other. The deliberate but hidden 'strategic' and 'ethnic' agendas of the government of Sudan have also come to play [an] increasing role in fuelling the conflict. Rather than taking concrete steps to ease ethnic tension and or resolving the resource conflict, the government of President El-Bashir, as did its predecessors, is largely seen to have been taking enraging steps by arming Arabs and their militia (Janjaweed) at the detriment of defenceless farming communities. Certainly, the key antidote to the conflict in Darfur region lies in structural reform of the state's centre of power in its dealings with the peripheries: provision of social justice and security, equal development, non-partisan policy formulation and implementation as well as the use of dialogue, rather than state violence, in resolving dissent and rebellion.

Global Warming Caused the Conflict in Darfur

Stephan Faris

Stephan Faris is a freelance journalist who has written about Africa and the Middle East for Time *and the* New York Daily News; *he is the author of* Forecast: The Consequences of Climate Change, from the Amazon to the Arctic, from Darfur to Napa Valley. *In the following viewpoint, he argues that the conflict in Darfur has been caused by climate change, which has created drought conditions in the region. African and Arab herders in Darfur used to live peacefully, he says, but with the drought, there are not enough resources for both, which has led to violence. He concludes that the West has a responsibility to help Darfur, since Western energy use has helped create climate change and cause the crisis.*

To truly understand the crisis in Darfur—and it has been profoundly misunderstood—you need to look back to the mid-1980s, before the violence between African and Arab began to simmer. Alex de Waal, now a program director at the Social Science Research Council, was there at that time, as a doctoral candidate doing anthropological fieldwork. Earlier this year, he told me a story that, he says, keeps coming back to him.

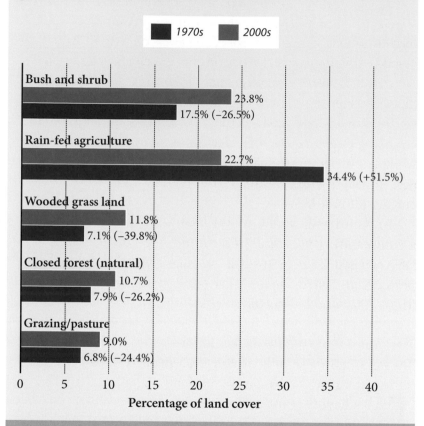

ENVIRONMENTAL IMPACT OF CLIMATE CHANGE IN SUDAN

Darfur's population increased from 1.3 million in 1973 to 6.5 million in 2003, further burdening the shrinking amount of arable land, grazing pastures, and water resources.

1970s   2000s

Bush and shrub
23.8%
17.5% (−26.5%)

Rain-fed agriculture
22.7%
34.4% (+51.5%)

Wooded grass land
11.8%
7.1% (−39.8%)

Closed forest (natural)
10.7%
7.9% (−26.2%)

Grazing/pasture
9.0%
6.8% (−24.4%)

0   5   10   15   20   25   30   35   40

Percentage of land cover

Source: "Darfur: Relief in a Vulnerable Environment," Tearfund, March 2007, p. 53. www.tearfund.org.

De Waal was traveling through the dry scrub of Darfur, studying indigenous reactions to the drought that gripped the region. In a herders' camp near the desert's border, he met with a bedridden and nearly blind Arab sheikh named Hilal Abdalla, who said he was noticing things he had never seen before: Sand blew into fertile land, and the rare rain washed away alluvial soil. Farmers who had once hosted his tribe and his camels were now blocking their migration; the land could no longer support both herder and farmer. Many tribesmen had lost their stock and scratched at millet farming on marginal plots.

The God-given order was broken, the sheikh said, and he feared the future. "The way the world was set up since time immemorial was being disturbed," recalled de Waal. "And it was bewildering, depressing. And the consequences were terrible."

In 2003, another scourge, now infamous, swept across Darfur. Janjaweed fighters in military uniforms, mounted on camels and horses, laid waste to the region. In a campaign of ethnic cleansing targeting Darfur's blacks, the armed militiamen raped women, burned houses, and tortured and killed men of fighting age. Through whole swaths of the region, they left only smoke curling into the sky.

At their head was a 6-foot-4 Arab with an athletic build and a commanding presence. In a conflict the United States would later call genocide, he topped the State Department's list of suspected war criminals. De Waal recognized him: His name was Musa Hilal, and he was the sheikh's son.

Farmers Versus Nomadic Herders

The fighting in Darfur is usually described as racially motivated, pitting mounted Arabs against black rebels and civilians. But the fault lines have their origins in another distinction, between settled farmers and nomadic herders fighting over failing lands. The aggression of the warlord Musa Hilal can be traced to the fears of his father, and to how climate change shattered a way of life.

Until the rains began to fail, the sheikh's people lived amicably with the settled farmers. The nomads were welcome passers-through, grazing their camels on the rocky hillsides that separated the fertile plots. The farmers would share their wells, and the herders would feed their stock on the leavings from the harvest. But with the drought, the farmers began to fence off their land—even fallow land—for fear it would be ruined by passing herds. A few tribes drifted elsewhere or took up farming, but the Arab herders stuck to their fraying livelihoods—nomadic herding was central to their cultural identity. (The distinction between "Arab" and "African" in Darfur is defined more by lifestyle than any physical difference: Arabs are generally herders, Africans typically farmers. The two groups are not racially distinct.)

The name *Darfur* means "Land of the Fur" (the largest single tribe of farmers in Darfur), but the vast region holds the tribal lands—the *dars*—of many tribes. In the late 1980s, landless and increasingly desperate Arabs began banding together to wrest their own *dar* from the black farmers. In 1987, they published a manifesto of racial superiority, and clashes broke out between Arabs and Fur. About 3,000 people, mostly Fur, were killed, and hundreds of villages and nomadic camps were burned before a peace agreement was signed in 1989. More fighting in the 1990s entrenched the divisions between Arabs and non-Arabs, pitting the Arab pastoralists against the Fur, Zaghawa, and Massaleit farmers. In these disputes, Sudan's central government, seated in Khartoum, often supported the Arabs politically and sometimes provided arms.

In 2003, a rebellion began in Darfur—a reaction against Khartoum's neglect and political marginalization of the region. And while the rebels initially sought a pan-ethnic front, the schism between those who opposed the government and those who supported it broke largely on ethnic lines. Even so, the conflict was rooted more in land envy than in ethnic hatred. "Interestingly, most of the Arab tribes who have their own land rights did not join the government's fight," says David Mozersky, the International Crisis Group's project director for the Horn of Africa.

Root Causes of the Drought

Why did Darfur's lands fail? For much of the 1980s and '90s, environmental degradation in Darfur and other parts of the Sahel (the semi-arid region just south of the Sahara) was blamed

Herders and livestock during a famine in 1997 in Darfur. The famines that struck the Darfur region may have added to tensions that resulted in the conflict of the early 2000s. © Liba Taylor/Robert Harding/Newscom.

on the inhabitants. Dramatic declines in rainfall were attributed to mistreatment of the region's vegetation. Imprudent land use, it was argued, exposed more rock and sand, which absorb less sunlight than plants, instead reflecting it back toward space. This cooled the air near the surface, drawing clouds downward and reducing the chance of rain. "Africans were said to be doing it to themselves," says Isaac Held, a senior scientist at the National Oceanic and Atmospheric Administration.

But by the time of the Darfur conflict four years ago, scientists had identified another cause. Climate scientists fed historical sea-surface temperatures into a variety of computer models of atmospheric change. Given the particular pattern of ocean-temperature changes worldwide, the models strongly predicted a disruption in African monsoons. "This was not caused by people cutting trees or overgrazing," says Columbia University's Alessandra Giannini, who led one of the analyses. The roots of the drying of Darfur, she and her colleagues had found, lay in changes to the global climate.

The extent to which those changes can be blamed on human activities remains an open question. Most scientists agree that greenhouse gases have warmed the tropical and southern oceans. But just how much artificial warming—as opposed to natural drifts in oceanic temperatures—contributed to the drought that struck Darfur is as debatable as the relationship between global warming and the destruction of New Orleans. "Nobody can say that Hurricane Katrina was definitely caused by climate change," says Peter Schwartz, the co-author of a 2003 Pentagon report on climate change and national security. "But we can say that climate change means more Katrinas. For any single storm, as with any single drought, it's difficult to say. But we can say we'll get more big storms and more severe droughts."

With countries across the region and around the world suffering similar pressures, some see Darfur as a canary in the coal mine, a foretaste of climate-driven political chaos. Environmental degradation "creates very dry tinder," says de Waal. "So if anyone wants to put a match to it, they can light it up." Combustion might be particularly likely in areas where the political or social geography is already fragile. "Climate change is likely to cause tension all over the world," says Idean Salehyan, a political scientist at the University of North Texas. Whether or not it sparks conflict, he says, depends on the strength, goodwill, and competence of local and national governments. . . .

In Darfur itself, recognizing climate change as a player in the conflict means seeking a solution beyond a political treaty between the rebels and the government. "One can see a way of de-escalating the war," says de Waal. "But unless you get at the underlying roots, it'll just spring back." One goal of the internationally sponsored peace process is the eventual return of locals to their land. But what if there's no longer enough decent land to go around?

A Long-Term and International Process

To create a new status quo, one with the moral authority of the God-given order mourned by Musa Hilal's father, local leaders would have to put aside old agreements and carve out new ones. Lifestyles and agricultural practices would likely need to change to accommodate many tribes on more fragile land. Widespread investment and education would be necessary.

But with Khartoum uncooperative, creating the conditions conducive to these sorts of solutions would probably require not only forceful foreign intervention but also a long-term stay. Environmental degradation means the local authorities have little or no surplus to use for tribal buy-offs, land deals, or coalition building. And fighting makes it nearly impossible to rethink land ownership or management. "The first thing you've got to do is stop the carnage and allow moderates to come to the fore," says Thomas Homer-Dixon, a political scientist at the University of Toronto. Yet even once that happens, he admits, "these processes can take decades."

Among the implications arising from the ecological origin of the Darfur crisis, the most significant may be moral. If the region's collapse was in some part caused by the emissions from our factories, power plants, and automobiles, we bear some responsibility for the dying. "This changes us from the position of Good Samaritans—disinterested, uninvolved people who may feel a moral obligation—to a position where we, unconsciously and without malice, created the conditions that led to this crisis," says Michael Byers, a political scientist at the University of British Columbia. "We cannot stand by and look at it as a situation of discretionary involvement. We are already involved."

Climate Change—Only One Cause Among Many for Darfur Conflict

IRIN

IRIN is a news service of the United Nations focusing on humanitarian issues. The following viewpoint argues that climate change may be one important aspect of the conflict in Darfur but cautions against oversimplifying a complex situation. IRIN says that the conflict has a range of causes that include historical animosities between groups, desire for equitable power sharing in government, and the absence of a democratic process. The viewpoint also explains that the conflict itself causes adverse effects on the environment in Sudan. According to the authors, reducing the situation in Darfur to a single cause may result in serious misunderstandings and make resolving the conflict more difficult.

Climate change may be one of the causes of the Darfur crisis, but to consider it the single root cause would obscure other important factors and could hamper the search for solutions, climate and conflict analysts say.

A number of commentators, journalists and analysts have recently focused on competition for natural resources, increasingly scarce due to global warming, as the trigger of the conflict in western Sudan.

"It [global warming] has become such a trendy issue that everything is being packaged as climate change," said Sorcha O'Callaghan, a researcher at the UK-based Overseas Development Institute (ODI).

"Competition for resources has definitely been one of the main issues in the conflict, but undue emphasis on it, at the expense of other causes, is an attempt to simplify the crisis. The complexity of the different factors driving Darfur's conflict need to be borne in mind in efforts towards its resolution and, therefore, over-simplification should be avoided," she added.

Blaming Climate Change

Among the earliest commentators to put a global warming spin on the Darfur crisis was economist Jeffrey Sachs. "Recent years have shown that shifts in rainfall can bring down governments and even set off wars. The African Sahel, just south of the Sahara, provides a dramatic and poignant demonstration," he wrote in an article on the *Scientific American* website in July last year.

"The deadly carnage in Darfur, Sudan, for example, which is almost always discussed in political and military terms, has roots in an ecological crisis directly arising from climate shocks," Sachs wrote.

A report on how climate change posed a threat to global security was produced earlier this year for the think-tank, CNA Corporation, by a group of former US military officials.

"Darfur provides a case study of how existing marginal situations can be exacerbated beyond the tipping point by climate-related factors. It also shows how lack of essential resources threatens not only individuals and their communities but also the region and the international community at large," the report commented.

In an opinion piece for the *Washington Post* earlier this month, UN Secretary-General Ban Ki-moon wrote, "Amid the diverse social and political causes, the Darfur conflict began as an ecological crisis, arising at least in part from climate change."

Sudan—Conflict Since Independence

In its 50 years of independence, Africa's largest country has been plagued by conflicts rooted, many historians say, in the economic, political, social and military domination of the country by a narrow elite within northern Sudan.

Civil war has touched the ten southern states, also the west (all three Darfur states), the centre (Blue Nile and Southern Kordofan states), the east (Kassala State) and the northeast (Red Sea State).

"Fighting in Darfur has occurred intermittently for at least thirty years. Until 2003, it was mostly confined to a series of partly connected tribal and local conflicts . . . [then] these hostilities escalated into a full-scale military confrontation in all three Darfur states, which also frequently spills into neighbouring Chad and the Central African Republic," according to a new report, Sudan: Post-Conflict Environmental Assessment, by the UN Environment Programme (UNEP).

A Range of Causes

Understanding all the causes of the Darfur crisis may need a more nuanced approach. Julie Flint, who with Alex de Waal, wrote the book *Darfur: The Short History of a Long War*, told IRIN, "There is some truth in this [the link between conflict and the demand for natural resources]. The great drought and famine of 1984–85 led to localised conflicts that generally pitted pastoralists against farmers in a struggle for diminishing resources, culminating in the Fur-Arab war of 1987–89."

But attempts to paint the Darfur conflict as simply resource-based "whitewashes the Sudan government", claimed Flint. The "full-fledged tragedy" starting in 2003, was caused by the government's response to the rebellion, "for which two people have already been indicted for war crimes by the ICC [International Criminal Court]—not by resource conflict".

The ODI's O'Callaghan listed a range of causes for the conflict, none of which a sole or primary cause: "Historical grievances, local perceptions of race, demands for a fair sharing of power between different groups, the inequitable distribution of economic resources and benefits, disputes over access to and control over increasingly scarce natural resources (land, livestock and water), the proliferation of arms and the militarisation of young people, the absence of a democratic process and other governance issues. . . . Local issues have been politicised and militarised, and drawn into the wider political dynamics of Sudan," she commented.

Geoffrey Dabelko, director of the Environmental Change and Security Programme at the Washington-based Woodrow Wilson International Center for Scholars, noted that "competition between pastoralists and agriculturalists is key to so many

A burned and abandoned village in Darfur is seen in an aerial view from 2004. Fighting in Darfur was often characterized by such scorched earth campaigns, with widespread destruction of the natural environment and the displacement of fleeing victims. © Majority World/UIG via Getty Images.

conflicts in East Africa, including the crisis in Darfur. Violence between tribes and ethnic groups are the most visible dividing lines, but the stories of these conflicts cannot be told without including underlying environmental and demographic stresses."

The Climate Change Factor

Sudan, along with other countries in the Sahel belt, has suffered several long and devastating droughts in the past few decades, the UNEP assessment pointed out. The most severe drought occurred in 1980–1984, and was accompanied by widespread displacement and localised famine.

The UNEP report also listed the erosion of natural resources caused by climate change as among the root causes of social strife and conflict.

"The scale of historical climate change, as recorded in Northern Darfur, is almost unprecedented: the reduction in rainfall has turned millions of hectares of already marginal semi-desert grazing land into desert. The impact of climate change is considered to be directly related to the conflict in the region, as desertification has added significantly to the stress on the livelihoods of pastoralist societies, forcing them to move south to find pasture," the report states.

Muawia Shaddad, of the Sudan Environment Conservation Society, told IRIN from Khartoum that data collected since 1917 in El Fasher, capital of North Darfur, showed that the average annual rainfall had halved. "But when we say that the conflicts started because of resources we are not denying the government did not make massive errors, and ethnicity had no role to play: all these things found a fertile soil in a situation which was already tense because of the demand for resources."

The UNEP report, too, acknowledges that many elements contributing to the conflict in Sudan have little or no link to the environment or natural resources. These include political, religious, ethnic, tribal and clan divisions, economic influences, land tenure deficiencies and historical feuds. "In addition, where environment and natural resource management issues are important, they are generally contributing factors only—not the sole cause for tension."

The Simplification Trap

Dabelko, of the Woodrow Wilson Center, commented: "The challenge is to avoid over-simplistic or deterministic formulations that equate climate change inexorably with genocide or terrorism, as some less careful commentators have done."

O'Callaghan also challenged commentators who "simplistically portrayed the Darfur conflict as an ethnic struggle between Arabs and Africans." "With political and military allegiances shifting between different groups, there is now greater acceptance that this does not adequately reflect the roots of the conflict," she said.

UNEP has identified categories of natural resources that have been linked to the various conflicts in Sudan: oil and gas reserves; Nile water; hardwood timber; rangeland and rain-fed agricultural land, and the associated water points.

The UN agency also considers the pastoralists versus agriculturalists theory simplistic. "The rural ethnic and livelihood structures of Sudan are so complex and area-specific that any summary of the issue of resource competition on a national scale is, by definition, a gross simplification. For instance, traditional pastoralist and agricultural societies in Sudan are not always clearly separated: in many areas, societies (families, clans and even whole tribes) practice a mixture of crop-growing and animal-rearing."

The report divides the groups into predominantly sedentary crop-rearing societies/tribes; nomadic livestock-rearing societies/tribes; and owners of, and workers in, mechanised agricultural schemes. The three groups depend all on rainfall for their livelihood.

Most of the recorded local conflicts take place within and between the first two groups, according to UNEP. The third

Refugee Camps and Firewood

In Darfur, over one-third of the population has been displaced by the ongoing conflicts, and many more are directly affected by this population displacement. As a result, many refugee camps have been established in the Darfur region. Yet these refugee camps are beneficial to the Sudan government because they attract relief aid and create a pool of recruits for the Sudanese army and cheap labour.

Land degradation and water and firewood scarcity are serious problems around large camps in Darfur, as is poor sanitation. Conditions continue to deteriorate in 2012; camps are crowded, and many refugees suffer from acute malnutrition and infectious diseases such as yellow fever and malaria. Tensions run high over access to scarce resources within the camps, there is constant danger of conflicts with neighbouring communities, and women and children face sexual violence when they leave the camps in search of firewood. The camps are recruiting grounds for various factions and militias. Loss of traditional family and societal structure, poverty, and trauma have resulted in increased violence in the camps, from rape to extortion. Individuals in positions of power and celebrity, such as actor George Clooney, have tried to draw attention to the plight of the Darfurian people, but still the problems persist.

Shirley A. Fedorak, Anthropology Matters, *second edition. Toronto, Ontario: University of Toronto Press, 2013, p. 72.*

group—the mechanised farming group—is generally not directly involved in conflict, but has played a very strong role in precipitating it in some states, by uncontrolled land grabs from the other two groups.

"[In the] Nuba Mountains and in Blue Nile State, combatants reported that the expansion of mechanised agricultural schemes onto their land had precipitated the fighting, which had then escalated, and coalesced with the major north-south political conflict."

Throughout Sudan's recorded history, pastoralists resisting the shrinkage and degradation of rangelands have been at the centre of local conflicts: competing with other groups for choice grazing land; moving and grazing livestock on cropland without consent; reducing competition by forcing other pastoralists and agriculturalists off previously shared land, said the UN agency's report.

In the Um Chelluta region of Southern Darfur, rain-fed agricultural land increased by 138 percent between 1973 and 2000, while rangeland decreased by 56 percent and closed woodland shrank by 32 percent. UNEP warned that the historical, ongoing, and forecast shrinkage and degradation of remaining rangelands in the northern part of the Sahel belt was set to exacerbate the situation.

A Vicious Cycle

Conflict, in its turn, is taking its toll on the environment. UNEP pointed out that the fighting in Darfur was often characterised by a 'scorched earth' campaign, carried out by militias over large areas, which not only resulted in a significant number of civilian deaths, but the widespread destruction of villages and forests, and the displacement of victims fleeing to camps for protection, food and water.

So environmental degradation is one of the driving forces of displacement and, according to UNEP, the environment is being further undermined by the sheer number of displaced people and refugees.

The environmental impact of a refugee or displacement camp is often high: UNEP researchers in Darfur found that extensive deforestation could be found as far as 10km from a camp; in some the situation was being aggravated by brick-making.

"One large tree is needed to provide the fire to make around 3,000 bricks. In addition, the clay needed for brick-making can damage trees by exposing roots, and also create pits in which water collects and mosquitoes can thrive," the UN agency warned.

"It is possible that some camps in Darfur will run out of viable fuel wood supplies within walking distance, resulting in major fuel shortages."

The UNEP report made recommendations to control and address the situation, including investment in environmental management, climate adaptation measures; capacity building of national and local government in environmental affairs, and the integration of environmental factors in all UN relief and development projects.

"The total cost of this report's recommendations is estimated at approximately US$120 million over three to five years. These are not large figures when compared to the Sudanese GDP in 2005 of $85.5 billion."

CHAPTER 3

Personal Narratives

Chapter Exercises

1. **Writing Prompt**

   Imagine that you are a refugee from Darfur requesting asylum. Write a letter describing your experiences in your home community and your reasons for fleeing. Include any relevant details about your life before the violence and how the crisis affected you personally. Describe what you hope to find in your host country and your hopes for the future of Darfur.

2. **Group Activity**

   Working in a small group, devise a questionnaire that could be used by a humanitarian aid worker to process new arrivals at a Darfuri refugee camp. The questions should be designed to determine the types of assistance the individual may need. The answers should provide basic demographic information and a good understanding of the person's current emotional, physical, and medical state.

Surviving Darfur, an African Doctor's Memoir

Arlene Getz

Arlene Getz is an editor for the media conglomerate Thomson Reuters and was previously an editor for Newsweek. *In the following viewpoint, she reports on the memoir* Tears of the Desert *by Halima Bashir, a doctor from a Darfuri village. Bashir witnessed widespread rape and murder of children and adults in Darfur and was herself raped and beaten. Her book vividly portrays the crisis as well as the life of her tribe before the crisis. The viewpoint explains that Bashir (no relation to the president of Sudan) is a pseudonym: the doctor does not want to be identified because of the stigma of rape in her society. Bashir also discusses seeking asylum in Great Britain and her hope that her story will help promote justice in Darfur.*

Too often, atrocities blur into abstractions. The burned-out villages; the camps for the desperate displaced; the brutalized women—for all that we've seen, read and heard about Darfur, for all the celebrities who've adopted it as their own cause célèbre, it's still hard for us to get a real sense of the hideousness

Darfur human rights activist Dr. Halima Bashir speaks about Darfur after meeting with US president George W. Bush in 2008. © Chris Kleponis/AFP/Getty Images.

that has taken place there. Halima Bashir might be the person who finally pulls us through that barrier.

Bashir was 24 when the Sudanese soldiers came for her. By then, of course, she was already sadly familiar with her country's political tensions. As a village child sent to school in the city, she had been taunted by members of Sudan's Arab elite for being African. As a medical student, her studies were repeatedly disrupted when the authorities closed down her campus and tried to force students to fight in what she called the "plastic jihad" against non-Muslim Sudanese in the south. But it was when she first saw the bleeding bodies of the 8-year-old girls from the school in the remote Darfuri village of Mazkhabad that she realized "someone had let the devil in" to her country.

Bashir was the lone doctor at the village clinic as teachers and parents carried the girls in. The Arab militia known as the Janjaweed had held some 40 of the children hostage for two hours, forcing them to watch as their friends were raped, beating them in the head with sticks or rifle butts if they tried to resist and yelling at them that Sudan was for Arabs, not black dogs and slaves. Bashir wept as she sutured, trying to comfort the girls and console herself that at least they were too young to become pregnant. "I eased little Aisha's legs open, to reveal a red, bloodied rawness," Bashir writes in her newly-released memoir *Tears of the Desert*. "When that first Arab had forced himself into her, he had ripped her apart. . . . It was exactly as I had expected, exactly what I had been fearing. I would have to clean the wound and sew her up again, and I knew that I had no anesthetic with which to do so."

It was a week later that the three men in dirty soldiers' uniforms dragged her off. Furious that she had given U.N. officials details about the attack on the village school, they beat her and left her tied and gagged in a hut at a nearby military camp. That night, three more men arrived, slashing at her with a razor before forcing themselves on her. "The three of them took turns raping me, one after the other," she writes. "Once the third had finished, they started over again. And while doing so they burned me with their cigarettes and cut me with their blades." The assaults continued for two days. On the third, the men let her go, telling her they'd let her live so she could go and tell the world what rape was.

Bashir managed to flee back to her own tribal village. Five months later, the war came for her again. One December day, she recalls, five helicopters banked low over the settlement, the lead one spewing bright flashes and puffs of smoke. "An instant later, the huts beneath it exploded, mud and thatch and branches and bodies being thrown into the air," she writes. "In the distance beneath the helicopters a massed rank of horsemen swept forward, firing their guns and screaming as they smashed into the village." Those who were able fled into the forest. Shortly before sunset, they crept back to their burning homes. Those too old or too young to run were shot, burned or stabbed to death; at least one newborn baby was thrown into a fire. The men who stayed to defend the village—among them Bashir's father—were a pile of corpses in the marketplace.

Bashir's memoir is appearing at a pivotal time for Darfur. Three months ago, Luis Moreno-Ocampo, the prosecutor of the International Criminal Court requested a warrant for the arrest of Sudanese president Omar al-Bashir on charges of ten counts of genocide, crimes against humanity and war crimes. The ICC's three-judge Pre-Trial Chamber has yet to rule on whether to issue the warrant, but the issue has generated a heated controversy among Darfur activists who fear that the arrest of an incumbent president will further destabilize Sudan and exacerbate the danger facing displaced Darfuris and aid groups working in the area. For the feisty Moreno-Ocampo, the young doctor's account undercuts the argument that justice will have to wait until there is peace in Sudan. "That's why Halima's book is so good," he told *Newsweek* in an interview. "It shows how rape is used as a silent weapon to destroy the Africans, to force them to have Arab children."

Bashir herself (no relation to the Sudanese president) supports the indictment too. But *Tears of the Desert* is far more than a litany of her pain. Indeed, much of its relevance lies in her account of her life *before* Darfur became a byword for genocide. Written together with veteran BBC journalist Damien Lewis, the book paints a vivid picture of a traditional lifestyle under siege, a portrait of the people of Darfur before they became victims. Bashir is Zaghawa, a member of a proud semi-nomadic tribe that can trace its roots back to the 7th century and that, together with other non-Arab Muslim tribes in Darfur, has been at the center of the conflict with the Janjaweed. Now 29, she grew up in a typical desert village. Home was a compound consisting of four circular mud huts surrounded by a fence made of tree branches. A chicken coop housed hens and pigeons, whose droppings were often mixed with oil to make a paste for injuries. Her days were spent playing with friends and helping a demanding grandmother with chores like collecting firewood or catching locusts for the frying pan. Traditional customs had to be observed: young children were cut on the face with a razor blade to form the distinctive scar patterning of the Zaghawa. Later, the girls marked their transition to womanhood through the searing pain of circumcision. Bashir had run away before her grandmother could scar her cheeks, but she couldn't escape the mutilation of the genital cutting—and her anger about it afterward.

That life is over now. Bashir's village is destroyed, its inhabitants either dead or in camps. Bashir herself managed to sell the family's hidden gold to buy herself passage to Britain. There she managed to find her husband, win political asylum and—in spite of the injuries sustained during the rape—give birth to two sons. By Darfur standards, she's enormously fortunate, but her tale is hardly a happy one. Her husband, also a Zaghawa who fled Darfur, still faces the threat of deportation from England. Her mother and sister, who fled the village ahead of her, face an uncertain future in a Chad refugee camp. She doesn't know the fate of her brothers.

Meanwhile, the fear of retaliation by the Sudanese government for telling her story forces her to protect her face and her identity. The name Halima Bashir is a pseudonym, she says, and she is afraid to be photographed with her face unveiled. The stigma her society attaches to rape also lingers; some of her remaining family is angry that she has told the world about it. Nonetheless, Bashir believes the risk and pain of publicity was necessary. "I'm writing my story for the people who can't write it for themselves," she told *Newsweek* during a recent visit to New York. "We need to move past the political and focus on the personal." In the end, that may be the only way to fully grasp the ghastliness of Darfur.

A Translator Describes the Violence in Darfur

Chris McCann

Chris McCann is a writer for PopMatters. *In the following viewpoint, he reviews Daoud Hari's* The Translator, *a memoir in which Hari describes his work as a translator for Western investigators in Darfur during the genocide. Hari interviewed many victims of the genocide and was himself kidnapped by militias. Hari feels that telling about his experiences can help Westerners understand what happened in Darfur. In McCann's view, Hari's personal stories will inspire readers to take positive action against genocide.*

The stories that emerge from genocidal societies are by definition incredible. That was the lesson the Holocaust should have taught us. In case after case of genocide, accounts that sounded far-fetched and that could not be independently verified repeatedly proved true.

> —*Samantha Power*, A Problem from Hell: America and the Age of Genocide

I bring the stories to you because I know most people want others to have good lives, and, when they understand the situation, they will do what they can to steer the world back toward kindness.

—*Daoud Hari,* The Translator: A Tribesman's Memoir of Darfur

The stories told in Daoud Hari's slim memoir, *The Translator*, are indeed incredible. So incredible that it's impossible at times to imagine them. The rape and mutilation of thousands upon thousands of women. The butchering of children. The destruction of villages, lives, and ways of life. It's easy to imagine, however, that you've heard them before. After some time, the atrocities we read about in the newspaper begin to blur. For Westerners, everything in Darfur seems so far away.

And with distance comes a softening of focus, a creeping indifference, and a casual forgetfulness. In *A Problem From Hell: America and the Age of Genocide* her excellent study of the American response to genocide in the 20th century, Samantha Power posits that one of the reasons the United States did so little to stop the slaughters in Turkey, Germany, Cambodia, Bosnia, and Rwanda is "a reluctance to imagine the unimaginable because of the consequences." Daoud Hari doesn't leave much to the imagination in his descriptions of what continues to take place in Darfur; his refusal to turn away is what makes *The Translator* such an important book.

Helping to Investigate Genocide

Hari was born in Darfur. He lived in a small village with his brothers and sisters and had a camel, Kelgi, as a pet. When he was 13, a detachment of the Sudanese Army came to his village looking for rebels. Understanding that it was no longer safe, his family sent him to the largest city in North Darfur, El Fasher, to finish school. There, and in his subsequent work in Libya and

Egypt, Hari learned to speak the English and Arabic that allowed him to be a translator for the UN and US-backed effort to determine whether what was happening in Darfur could be classified as genocide.

As a Sudanese citizen who took reporters into the Darfur region, Hari was in constant danger of arrest, imprisonment, and execution for treason. Still, he returned again and again to show people what had happened to the land of his youth. "This part of the world, our world, was changing so quickly every day, falling deeper into the fires of cruelty. I wanted to wake up from it." He describes how persistent drought conditions have made a hard land even harder. The reduction in resources allowed the Islamic government of the north to foment unrest among nomadic Arabs in the south, providing them with arms and encouraging them to wipe out the native tribespeople with whom they had lived in peace for generations. As a result of government pressure, Hari says, neighbors are massacring neighbors and villages are ravaged by brutality, fear, and death.

Often, he asks his readers to put themselves in his place. "Imagine if all the systems and rules that held your country together fell apart suddenly and your family members were all—every one of them—in a dangerous situation." It's a simple ploy and is amazingly effective. It's as though Hari is right there trying to explain the unexplainable to someone he believes will understand if given enough information.

Understated Stories of Terrible Events

The unembellished prose throughout the book is also reminiscent of solid journalism. Hari tells the stories as they are told to (and through) him. He recalls his first days in a refugee camp in Chad, translating for the genocide investigators who wanted to interview those who made it out of Darfur, out of their villages, out of their lives, alive. ". . . the stories came pouring out, and often they were set before us slowly and quietly like tea. These slow stories were told with understatement that made my eyes and voice fill as I translated; for when people seem to have no emotion remaining for such stories, your own heart must supply it." There are many times in Hari's own account when the reader is called upon to do just that.

When the stories Hari tells are so terrible, so "incredible", the language he uses becomes thinner and more transparent until it recedes into the background and allows the events to dominate the page. At these moments, the distance between reader and story collapses so dramatically that there is no escape. One cannot avoid being thrust into what, just moments before, was only a narrative. "The first day was very hard on everyone who told a story and everyone who listened. . . . The coming days would be no easier."

After the US declared the situation in Darfur a genocide, Hari continued to escort reporters (mostly from the UK and the US) into increasingly dangerous areas. He purchased a cell phone with the stipend he received for the translation work he did with the genocide investigators, and he prided himself on knowing which rebel groups were in control of which areas and who to call to ensure safe passage for himself and his charges. But as the border region grew increasingly chaotic, who was in charge became harder and harder to determine. One day, Hari, a *National Geographic* reporter named Paul, and Ali, their driver, were captured.

The last half of the book follows the three prisoners as they make the terrifying rounds of various commanders, child soldiers, and filthy prison cells. This Kafkaesque odyssey illuminates another aspect of the impossible situation in Darfur. Nobody knows who is in control; children tote Kalashnikovs and discuss torture, and people are killed for no reason other than the fact that they happened to be in the wrong place at the wrong time. If anything, Darfur these past years has been the epitome of "the wrong place", but as Hari maintains throughout the book, it wasn't always this way. From a Western vantage point, the situation can appear hopeless, the parties intractable, and the violence both horrific and inscrutable. But Hari believes that his homeland can return to the peaceful, rational place it once was. And after reading his own story, this belief has an indescribable poignancy.

Personal Stories That Inspire Action

In *A Problem From Hell*, Power argues that the silence of the Western world was another reason that 20th century genocides were allowed to continue without international intervention. I finished *The Translator* with the feeling that I needed to do something but I still wasn't sure what. "What can one person do?" Hari asks near the end of his story. He answers the rhetorical question in the same logical, hopeful (but not prescriptive) tone he somehow maintains throughout his journey. "You make friends, of course, and do what you can." It is this strict focus on the personal that in the end makes Hari's account of the hell that Darfur has become something more than just an exercise in despair.

Nobody agrees on exactly what to do, but that doesn't mean we should do nothing. At the very least, Hari believes, we should educate ourselves about what is happening. At one point in the story, Hari and two American reporters are trying to escape a furious Janjaweed militia attack on a village. There is no room for error. Hari says of the man at the wheel, upon whom their survival depended, "He was too nervous to be driving, but he was in the driver's seat." That is the case with us all. We might not be fit to drive, but there's no one else who can get us where we need to go.

The Translator is a short book. It is engagingly written. And it is absolutely essential reading if we are not to repeat the mistakes of the 20th century in the infancy of the 21st. If we all took an afternoon to read Daoud Hari's account of what is happening in Darfur, no government would be able to ignore the ocean of voices that would rise up in protest. That would be a story worth telling.

The Devil Came on Horseback: Bearing Witness to the Genocide in Darfur

Brian Steidle and Gretchen Steidle Wallace

Brian Steidle is a former US Marine Corps captain and a military and security operations expert. Gretchen Steidle Wallace, Steidle's sister, is the founder of the nonprofit organization Global Grassroots and a producer of the documentary They Came on Horseback, *a film about Steidle's tenure as an American observer in Darfur. In the following viewpoint, Steidle discusses his work in Darfur. He describes witnessing Arab militias inflict serious injuries on an African infant. He presents this experience as indicative of the genocidal violence in Darfur abetted by the government of Sudan.*

The rains had already moved on, leaving a dry, oppressive heat that threatened to bake any creature moving too slowly beneath the sun. It was about 115 degrees Fahrenheit. As I disembarked from our helicopter, I breathed as deeply as I could without frying my lungs, steadied myself, and, blinking, took a look around. Camel-colored dust stretched before us as far as we could see.

Ahmed and I headed toward a large nim tree on the outskirts of Wash al Tool, where 250 homeless women and children had stopped earlier in the day to share in the small piece of shade. They had escaped the initial conflict in Alliet, a town of 15,000 we had just visited. The village was the most recent to fall prey to Government of Sudan troops in what was now described by Western diplomats—publicly, if belatedly—as genocide.

Had anyone been injured? We had to ask, even though we were all but certain of the answer. Expressionless, a woman slowly raised a one-year-old girl for me to examine, as if I were a doctor with miracle cures. I quickly took a photo to document the injury before motioning for her to put the child down. I examined the baby, gently directing the woman to move the child this way or that so we could understand her wounds. I realized my instructions only confirmed her presumption that I was a medical professional. I felt increasingly helpless.

The baby's breathing was labored, and she was wheezing noticeably. Upon closer inspection, I realized that this tiny human being had been shot in the back—the child had gaping entry and exit wounds that accentuated her struggle to breathe. Her guardian looked up at me with a blank gaze.

"What's her name?" I stammered, my sense of disbelief audible in my tone.

"Mihad Hamid," she said after a quick translation of my question. The woman, Mihad's aunt, explained that while the child's mother was running from the Government of Sudan troops, carrying the wrapped child on her back, Mihad had been wounded. Attempting to protect both Mihad and her three-year-old brother, Oman, their mother perished in the attack. I was shocked at the lack of emotion in this woman who had just lost her sister and who by default was now this infant's keeper.

Mihad also had received a shrapnel wound on the right side of her head. Round bloody gashes speckled the baby's scalp. Oman lay nestled in the lap of another woman, perhaps a relative or perhaps a mother who had lost her own children in this brutal assault. The woman carefully placed Oman on the ground on his stomach to show us his wounds. Someone had whipped him on the left side of his neck, and I could see a marble-sized shrapnel wound on his buttocks. Both children lay quietly despite their injuries—innocent victims of a ruthless conflict we still could not fully comprehend.

"Captain Brian! Now see what they do here!" Ahmed screamed full of rage at what we had just seen. Ahmed, the Chadian mediator for our African Union monitoring team, was a decorated soldier who had served as a rebel in his own country's civil war. Almost always smiling, he was a compact force of African muscle, confidence, and integrity. Ahmed fulfilled his official duties as a mediator with strict impartiality regardless of the situation, yet he had no fear of confrontation, if it was necessary, when we met up with the Arab nomad militias or their enablers—the soldiers and officials of the Government of Sudan.

I shook my head and swallowed with half-hearted acceptance that there was nothing I could say or do to change the situation. I took photos and made notes for my report. Silently fuming, I moved on clutching my camera a little too fiercely.

I thought back to where I was a year before. I had just completed my term of service in the US Marine Corps, during which I'd served in Kosovo as part of the NATO mission policing villages and prohibiting arms trafficking from Macedonia. After leaving the Marine Corps, I was still eager to be involved somewhere in the field, using my military background. I thought it was a miracle when a civilian contracting company offered me a position in Sudan; it just didn't seem possible at the time that someone would pay me a six-figure salary to hang out in an exotic part of Africa, drive Land Cruisers around in the desert, and, as a civilian, advise a military operation. I accepted the mission with the enthusiasm of a boy invited to Disney World for the first time.

I wasn't completely naïve. I knew there would be conflict. Mass murder in the name of God or national and ethnic superiority had been an unfortunate reality of human life long before the birth of Jesus or Mohammed. Over centuries we have advanced technologically, and yet we still kill each other. It's something that never changes. In the last century alone, genocide was commonplace—Turks killing more than a million Armenians in 1915, the Nazi slaughter of 6 million Jews during the Holocaust, Indonesia's purge of hundreds of thousands of real and imagined Communists in the '60s, the massacres by the Khmer Rouge in Cambodia in the '70s and '80s, and tribe-on-tribe slaughter in Rwanda in 1994.

Now, a decade after Rwanda, it was happening again in Africa. Still, I never expected to see first-hand what I was now seeing in Darfur. Here was a country in the early twenty-first century run by a government that condoned slavery, that used rape as a weapon of war, and that was indiscriminate in its attacks on its enemies. American forces are trained to avoid civilian casualties at all cost. Here, before my eyes, civilians—men, women, and children—were equal targets of the Government of Sudan. This was genocide, up close and personal. I couldn't reconcile or even remotely justify what had happened in Alliet.

A limited African Union monitoring force of 300 and an additional 1,700 soldiers for protection had been assigned to the Darfur region of Sudan where fighting had broken out in early 2003. An initial uprising among black African tribes seeking greater rights had been quickly squelched by the oppressive, Arab-led Government of Sudan. The government took the occasion to dig deeper trenches between the African farming villages and the Arab nomadic herders of Darfur. By arming the Arab nomads, the Government of Sudan had orchestrated a bloody campaign of terror to wipe out the black ethnic groups and permanently alter the demography of the region. Civilians took up arms, often only using elephant spears and stolen weapons to protect their villages against the terrorists they called "the devil on a horse," or *Janjaweed*. By the time I arrived in Darfur, the conflict had reached the scale of civil war, and the United States had called it genocide.

Our mandate was to investigate and report on violations of the supposed ceasefire agreement between the GOS and the two "rebel" groups, the Justice and Equality Movement and the Sudanese Liberation Army. My particular monitoring team of eight was one of only two observer teams operating in South Darfur, an area one-third the size of Texas. Our cast of characters included two African Union members from other African states, a representative of each of the three parties of the Darfur Ceasefire Agreement, a Chadian mediator, an interpreter, and one representative from the European Union or the United States who provided impartial logistical and technical expertise. I was one of only three American monitors assigned to all of Darfur. As unarmed observers, our mandate prohibited us from taking any further action to protect civilians or arrest and discipline perpetrators of the chaos. Our only official task was to observe, inquire, and write reports. While world leaders applauded this "African solution to an African problem," it was slowly becoming apparent that any effort on our part to contain the expanding violence served merely as a facade for what was a relatively inexperienced, ill-equipped, and under-resourced mission. It was an ironic predicament; though my military background as a former US Marine gave me a unique perspective on the limitations of the monitoring force, it was obvious that I was standing on a battlefield where no American had ever been trained to fight.

It had taken me nearly a month to convince the African Union to allow me to take photographs for our team in the field. I was an amateur who had developed a love of photography and felt that a visual record could be useful to our team. I was exhilarated by the idea of playing a role akin to a war photojournalist.

The African Union's skepticism was grounded in a previous leak to *60 Minutes* of photographs shot during a bloody attack on Suleia, where a girls' primary school had been destroyed. Somehow I convinced African Union officials that I was qualified and also committed to what some might consider a gruesome task, but one that I thought was a vital contribution to the history of this conflict. The photos were to be used as supplements to each report we submitted following an investigation of a ceasefire violation.

Before heading to Darfur, I went online to research the best tools of photojournalism and wound up purchasing an expensive, ten-pound digital camera with a serious 16-inch lens. When I finally held it in my hands—after a carefully engineered journey to Sudan across three continents, carried by a colleague from home— I almost trembled with excitement at the thought of whipping this new weapon out of my reporter's arsenal. It somehow compensated for the fact that the only other things I carried with me, besides a darkening suntan, were desert survival accoutrements— all non-lethal—including a canvas hat, sunglasses, water in my Camelbak, a pen and a waterproof notebook. But at first, I always reached for my smaller digital camera, which I considered less intrusive when faced with the crusted eyes of a wounded child or the downward glance of a woman recently assaulted by strangers.

Today in Wash al Tool, October 20, 2004, I lost my hesitation.

What kind of person can aim a gun at a one-year-old child?

If I wanted to capture evidence for whatever future cause, I was determined to make it the best damn evidence anyone had ever seen. And I would protect this photographic archive with my life. I swung my backpack around and retrieved my superior camera. It didn't feel quite like my old M-16, but somehow I felt more prepared for what I might uncover next.

We walked further into the village to speak with a few more wounded. Villagers directed us to two young girls, six-year-old Fatima Adouma Akhmed Ibrahim, who had been shot in the right foot, and eleven-year-old Salha Adouma Akhmed Ibrahim, who had been shot in her left thigh. Both were lying in makeshift cots, constructed of rough-cut logs and saw palmetto twine. One of the girl's legs had been placed in a wood splint and bandaged with fresh gauze—a rarity in these parts. I was struck by the remarkable resourcefulness of their guardians. I took the first few

US marine Brian Steidle conducts a press conference in March 2005 about his experiences in Darfur and shares photographs he took of seriously wounded children. © Tom Williams/Roll Call/Getty Images.

photographs for what would eventually evolve into a controversial campaign of evidence, espionage, advocacy, and threats to my career and my life.

Riding back in the helicopter that night, I felt shaken by what I had seen. It was still over 100 degrees, and we were sweating because no breeze came through the sealed windows. The stagnant air only added to the weight of the dismay. Sitting, stunned, in the backward-facing jump seat beside the latched door, I offered up my digital camera so my teammates could preview what I had just recorded.

At the sight of Milhad on the camera's screen, the Sudanese Liberation Army and Justice and Equality Movement representatives turned immediately to the Government of Sudan monitor and screamed at him in Arabic over the seats. Spittle sprayed from the Sudanese Liberation Army representative's lips as he gestured at my camera screen shoving it into the Government of

Sudan official's face so that he could see Mihad. Surprised, the government representative pressed himself back into his seat but said nothing. Ahmed jumped up to intervene. He shouted over the rebel monitors, bracing his arm against their chests, and retrieved my camera. The Government of Sudan representative turned away dismissively.

"We must handle this officially," Ahmed stated in English to the team as he handed me my camera. We rode the rest of the way in silence.

Back at home base in Myala, we notified the International Committee of the Red Cross and other nongovernmental organizations of the fighting, casualties, medical and emergency needs, and location of the displaced so that they could respond appropriately. Coordinating with humanitarian groups to treat the injured was not part of our mandate, but it was one of our regular practices. I specifically mentioned the condition of Mihad Hamid so that they might find her.

We attempted to return for a follow up visit over the next two days, but the Sudanese Liberation Army had amassed several hundred troops to attack the Government of Sudan and push it out of Alliet. Our unarmed monitoring team was unable to gain access to the town. Instead, we remained in our helicopter, sitting on the tarmac 200 kilometers away in Nyala and awaiting word that the fighting had stopped. We received reports via satellite phone from our Sudanese Liberation Army contact on the ground that Antonov aircraft were dropping bombs and that helicopter gunships were firing on the village to eliminate the remaining residents.

Despite the heavy fighting in the surrounding areas, Red Cross medics traveled courageously to within 20 kilometers of Alliet, facing gunfire, to treat victims of the attack. But they were never able to locate Mihad.

The greatest regret of my entire time in Darfur—in fact, of my life to this day—is not taking Mihad Hamid and her brother back to our headquarters for medical care. The African Union had not authorized us to help civilians, and bringing those children back with us did not occur to me until we landed back in Nyala. But it would have been the right thing to do.

Instead, I can at least offer this account of what I witnessed in Mihad's homeland, a faraway place where a government, abetted by others incited to hatred, is attempting to "cleanse" an entire people—where Arab Muslims kill African Muslims because the Africans are "too black." Darfur is more than an occasional headline in the newspaper or 20 seconds on a forgotten nightly newscast. It is where genocide continues to happen while the rest of the world goes through the motions of concern but does nothing of substance to stop it. Will the world ever wake up?

As of this writing, I do not know if Mihad Hamid survived.

Darfur Attack Survivors Tell of Brutal Killings

Opheera McDoom

Opheera McDoom is a journalist and Reuters correspondent who reports from Egypt and Sudan. In the following viewpoint, she shares eyewitness accounts about a Janjaweed raid on a market in 2010. According to survivor reports, the attackers rounded up village men and shot them. McDoom says that Darfur has descended into chaos, with rampant violence by militias and gangs, including kidnapping and attacks on aid workers. Doctors Without Borders was the only aid organization working in the town, and it was able to confirm the number of dead and injured, according to the author. Some humanitarian aid agencies were expelled by Sudanese president Omar al-Bashir, she writes, and there is little help for victims in Darfur.

Darfuri men were shot dead at point blank range during a surprise Arab militia raid on a busy market this month [September 2010] in which at least 39 people were killed and almost 50 injured, eyewitnesses said on Friday.

The attack on civilians was reminiscent of the early years of the counter-insurgency operation in Sudan's west, which took up arms against the government in 2003, complaining that the region had been neglected by Khartoum [Sudan].

The International Criminal Court [ICC] in The Hague [The Netherlands] has since issued an arrest warrant for Sudanese President Omar Hassan al-Bashir for genocide and war crimes in Darfur, charges he denies.

Details of the September 2 attack on the market in the village of Tabarat have not previously come to light. The government prevented peacekeepers from visiting the site until days later.

But five survivors of the attack told Reuters that heavily armed Arab militia had targeted male victims and shot many at point blank range.

Eyewitness Accounts

One diplomat said the militia were likely from among those armed and mobilized by the government to quell the rebels. Those militia, known as Janjaweed, were responsible for mass rape, murder and looting. Many of the tribal militia still support the government but Khartoum has lost control over some.

In Tabarat, men were rounded up by militia wearing military uniforms who rode into the market on horses and camels pretending to be buying goods before spraying the shops with gunfire. Then vehicles mounted with machine guns and carrying militia fighters appeared and rounded up some of the men, survivors said.

"They laid them down and they came up close and shot them in their heads," Abakr Abdelkarim, 45, told Reuters by telephone from the town of Tawilla, where many of the victims had sought refuge and medical help.

"(Those killed) were all men and one woman—some men were tied with rope behind the cars and dragged until they died."

Run for His Life

Adam Saleh said he had run for his life and hidden in nearby fields to watch from afar. "They were targeting men—all of them were shot in the head and chest, only those who were running away got shot in their legs and arms."

Nour Abdallah, 45, said the attackers let most of the women run away. She could not escape and so lay face down in the dirt. "They told me not to lift my head up or I would be shot too."

Saleh and others said after the attack they had gone to the joint U.N.–African Union (UNAMID) peacekeeping base in Tawilla to ask peacekeepers to come to Tabarat but they had refused.

"They also refused to come and help us recover the bodies," Saleh added.

UNAMID has said both rebels and the government prevented it getting access to the area.

Similar Reports from Other Witnesses

A UNAMID spokesman said he could not comment on the witness reports but an internal document seen by Reuters showed UNAMID had received similar witness reports of men being executed.

The only aid agency working in Tawilla, Médecins Sans Frontières [MSF, Doctors Without Borders], said it could confirm 39 people died and it had treated 46 injured, many with "serious gunshot wounds."

"We saw only men," said MSF head of mission Alessandro Tuzza. He said he could not comment on how the victims were shot but that MSF was still negotiating with the government to get access to the area in North Darfur province.

The witnesses said they had buried 41 bodies in common graves but more were still in the bushes around the market.

Sudan's army denied involvement in the attack and said the local government was investigating. "The North Darfur government have formed a security committee to investigate this."

Presidential adviser Ghazi Salaheddin visited the area on Friday on a fact-finding mission.

Kidnapping and violent banditry have become frequent in Darfur where years of impunity and the ready availability of arms have fueled a breakdown in law and order, with foreign workers targeted for abductions even in the main towns.

Bashir expelled 13 of the largest aid agencies working in Darfur after the ICC arrest warrant last year and many gaps in the humanitarian operation have yet to be filled.

"We are begging the international aid agencies to come and give us food, water. We have women and children here sitting in the sun for days with no shelter. We have nothing," said Abdelkarim.

Organizations to Contact

The editors have compiled the following list of organizations concerned with the issues debated in this book. The descriptions are derived from materials provided by the organizations. All have publications or information available for interested readers. The list was compiled on the date of publication of the present volume; the information provided here may change. Be aware that many organizations take several weeks or longer to respond to inquiries, so allow as much time as possible.

Amnesty International
5 Penn Plaza, 14th Floor
New York, NY 10001
(212) 807-8400 • fax: (212) 463-9193
e-mail: aimember@aiusa.org
website: www.amnestyusa.org

Amnesty International is a global human rights organization that seeks to promote and protect the basic rights of all individuals worldwide. It envisions a world in which every person enjoys all of the human rights enshrined in the Universal Declaration of Human Rights and other international human rights standards. It publishes reports on its advocacy work and human rights issues throughout the world. Amnesty International's website includes reports and news items, including a section on human rights in Sudan.

Embassy of the Republic of Sudan
2210 Massachusetts Ave.
Washington, DC 20008
(202) 338-8565 • fax: (202) 667-2406
website: www.sudanembassy.org

The website of the official representative of Sudan in the United States includes basic information about the country and its people, current news stories, photos, and visa information. The website also features a documents section where visitors may read and download the 2011 peace agreement with the Sudan People's Liberation Movement.

Genocide Watch
PO Box 809
Washington, DC 20044
(202) 643-1405
e-mail: communications@genocidewatch.org
www.genocidewatch.org

Genocide Watch aims to "predict, prevent, stop, and punish genocide and other forms of mass murder" by raising awareness of the eight-stage process of genocide and influencing international policy to curtail potential and actual acts of genocide. Its website includes news alerts and annual reports on countries at risk due to a growing likelihood of genocide or other atrocities. The website also offers links to reports issued by other members of the International Alliance to End Genocide, an international coalition of similar organizations coordinated through Genocide Watch.

Human Rights Watch
350 Fifth Ave., 34th Floor
New York, NY 10118-3299
(212) 290-4700 • fax: (212) 736-1300
e-mail: hrwnyc@hrw.org
website: www.hrw.org

Founded in 1978, this nongovernmental organization conducts systematic investigations of human rights abuses around the world and actively advocates for human dignity. It publishes books and reports on specific countries and issues, as well as annual reports and other articles. Its website includes numerous discussions of human rights and international justice issues, including a special section on Sudan.

Institute for the Study of Genocide (ISG)
John Jay College of Criminal Justice
899 Tenth Ave., Room 325
New York, NY 10019
e-mail: info@instituteforthestudyofgenocide.org
website: http://studyofgenocide.org

The ISG is an independent nonprofit organization established in 1982 that promotes and disseminates scholarship and policy analyses on the causes, consequences, and prevention of genocide. It publishes a semiannual newsletter and holds periodic conferences; maintains liaison with academic, human rights, and refugee organizations; provides consultation to representatives of media, governmental, and nongovernmental organizations; and advocates passage of legislation and administrative measures related to genocide and gross violations of human rights.

International Criminal Court (ICC)
PO Box 19519, 2500 CM
The Hague, The Netherlands
+31 (0)70 515 8515 • fax: +31 (0)70 515 8555
e-mail: visit@icc-cpi.int
website: www.icc-cpi.int

The ICC is a treaty-based international court established to try perpetrators of the most serious crimes of concern to the international community. Its website includes annual reports on the activities of the court, information about situations and cases, relevant legal texts, and other information.

Montreal Institute for Genocide and Human Rights Studies
Concordia University
1455 De Maisonneuve Blvd.

West Montreal, Quebec H3G 1M8, Canada
(514) 848-2424, ext. 5729 or 2404 • fax: (514) 848-4538
website: http://migs.concordia.ca

Founded in 1986, the Montreal Institute for Genocide and Human Rights Studies monitors native-language media for early warning signs of genocide in countries deemed to be at risk of mass atrocities and collects and disseminates research on the historical origins of mass killings. The institute houses the Will to Intervene Project, a research initiative focused on the prevention of genocide and other mass atrocities. The institute's website provides numerous links to information on genocide and related issues as well as specialized sites organized by nation, region, or case.

Prevent Genocide International (PGI)
1804 S Street, NW
Washington, DC 20009
(202) 483-1948 • fax: (202) 328-0627
e-mail: info@preventgenocide.org
website: www.preventgenocide.org

PGI is a global education and action network established in 1998 with the purpose of bringing about the elimination of genocide. In an effort to promote education on genocide, PGI maintains a multilingual website for the education of the international community. The website maintains a database of government documents and news releases as well as original content provided by members.

STAND
1800 Wyoming Ave. NW, Third Floor
Washington, DC 20036
(202) 643-7238
e-mail: info@standnow.org
website: www.standnow.org

STAND is a student-led organization that envisions a world in which the global community is willing and able to protect civilians from genocide and mass atrocities. In order to empower individuals and communities with the tools to prevent and stop genocide, STAND recommends activities from engaging government representatives to hosting fundraisers, and it has more than one thousand student chapters at colleges and high schools. STAND maintains many documents and other online resources and also provides plans for promoting action and education.

United to End Genocide
1010 Vermont Ave. NW, Suite 1100
Washington DC, 20005
(202) 556-2100
e-mail: info@endgenocide.org
website: http://endgenocide.org / http://savedarfur.org

United to End Genocide, which sponsors the Save Darfur project, was formed through the merger of several organizations that came about in response to the genocide in Darfur. Its mission focuses on ending genocide and mass atrocities worldwide through the actions of its diverse network of community activists, including genocide survivors. The Save Darfur project seeks to protect civilians in Darfur, promote peace, and hold genocide perpetrators accountable for their actions.

US Department of State
2201 C Street, NW
Washington, DC 20520
(202) 647-4000
website: www.state.gov

The US Department of State is the agency of the federal government responsible for foreign affairs. The website includes daily press briefings, reports on policy issues, and numerous other articles. The office of the historian includes historical information and documents related to the United States' relationship with Sudan.

World Without Genocide
William Mitchell College of Law
875 Summit Ave.
St. Paul, MN 55105
(651) 695-7621
e-mail: info@worldwithoutgenocide.org
website: http://worldwithoutgenocide.org

World Without Genocide works to protect innocent people around the world. It aims to fight racism and prejudice, advocate for the prosecution of perpetrators, and remember those whose lives and cultures have been destroyed by violence. Its website includes links to resources and discussions of numerous genocides and conflicts, including reports on Sudan and Darfur.

List of Primary Source Documents

The editors have compiled the following list of documents that either broadly address genocide and persecution or more narrowly focus on the topic of this volume. The full text of these documents is available from multiple sources in print and online.

Comprehensive Peace Agreement (CPA) Between Sudan and Southern Rebels, January 2005

Also known as the Naivasha Agreement, this agreement intended to end the second Sudan civil war when it was signed by the Sudan People's Liberation Movement and the government of Sudan. The CPA also addressed the development of a democratic government, the sharing of oil revenues, and a timetable for a referendum on independence by southern Sudan.

Convention Against Torture and Other Cruel, Inhuman, or Degrading Treatment or Punishment, United Nations, 1974

A draft resolution adopted by the UN General Assembly in 1974 opposing any nation's use of torture, unusually harsh punishment, and unfair imprisonment.

Convention on the Prevention and Punishment of the Crime of Genocide, December 9, 1948

A resolution of the UN General Assembly that defines genocide in legal terms and advises participating countries to prevent and punish actions of genocide in war and peacetime.

The Crisis in Darfur, Testimony Before the Senate Foreign Relations Committee, September 9, 2004

The text of a speech delivered by the US secretary of state Colin Powell in which he declares that the crisis in Darfur is a genocide and a situation that the international community must address.

Doha Document for Peace in Darfur, July 2011

Also known as the 2011 Darfur Peace Agreement, this document signed by the government of Sudan and the Liberation and Justice Movement established a compensation fund for victims of the Darfur conflict and a Darfur Regional Authority to oversee the region until a referendum is held to determine the area's permanent status.

Principles of International Law Recognized in the Charter of the Nuremberg Tribunal, United Nations International Law Commission, 1950

After World War II (1939–1945), the victorious Allies legally tried surviving leaders of Nazi Germany in the German city of Nuremberg. The proceedings established standards for international law that were affirmed by the United Nations and by later court tests. Among other standards, national leaders can be held responsible for crimes against humanity, which might include "murder, extermination, deportation, enslavement, and other inhuman acts."

Rome Statute of the International Criminal Court, July 17, 1998

The treaty that established the International Criminal Court. It establishes the court's functions, jurisdiction, and structure.

United Nations General Assembly Resolution 96 on the Crime of Genocide, December 11, 1946

A resolution of the UN General Assembly that affirms that genocide is a crime under international law.

Universal Declaration of Human Rights, United Nations, December 10, 1948

Soon after its founding, the United Nations approved this general statement of individual rights that it hoped would apply to citizens of all nations.

Warrant of Arrest for Omar Hassan Ahmad al-Bashir, March 4, 2009

The official document from the International Criminal Court states that there are reasonable grounds to believe that the president of Sudan is criminally responsible for war crimes and crimes against humanity under the Rome Statute.

Whitaker Report on Genocide, 1985

This report addresses the question of the prevention and punishment of the crime of genocide. It calls for the establishment of an international criminal court and a system of universal jurisdiction to ensure that genocide is punished.

For Further Research

Books

Hamid Eltgani Ali, *Darfur's Political Economy: A Quest for Development*. New York: Routledge, 2014.

Richard Cockett, *Sudan: Darfur, Islamism and the World*. New Haven, CT: Yale University Press, 2010.

Alex de Waal and Julie Flint, *Darfur: A New History of a Long War*, updated edition. London: Zed Books, 2012.

Steven Fake and Kevin Funk, *Scramble for Africa: Darfur-Intervention and the USA*. Tonawanda, NY: Black Rose Books, 2009.

John Hagan and Wenona Rymond-Richmond, *Darfur and the Crime of Genocide*. Cambridge, MA: Cambridge University Press, 2008.

Rebecca Hamilton, *Fighting for Darfur: Public Action and the Struggle to Stop Genocide*. London: Palgrave Macmillan, 2011.

Mukesh Kupila, *Against a Tide of Evil*. Sacramento, CA: Pegasus, 2013.

Andrew S. Natsios, *Sudan, South Sudan, and Darfur: What Everyone Needs to Know*. New York: Oxford University Press, 2012.

Gérard Prunier, *Darfur: A 21st-Century Genocide,* third edition. Ithaca, NY: Cornell University Press, 2011.

Samuel Totten, *An Oral and Documentary History of the Darfur Genocide*. Santa Barbara, CA: Praeger, 2010.

Periodicals

The Economist, "Sudan and Its Rebels: A Deal over Darfur?," February 3, 2011. www.economist.com.

Mia Farrow and Daniel Jonah Goldhagen, "Mass Slaughter and Obama's Mystifying Indifference," *Wall Street Journal*, September 26, 2013. http://online.wsj.com.

Jeffrey Gettleman, "A Taste of Hope Sends Refugees Back to Darfur," *New York Times*, February 26, 2012. www.nytimes.com.

Andrew Green, "Going South," *New Republic*, May 4, 2012. www.newrepublic.com.

Nat Hentoff, "Al-Bashir's Genocide Horrors Began and Continue in Darfur," Cato Institute, October 9, 2013. www.cato.org.

Human Rights Watch, "Sudan: ICC Warrant for Al-Bashir on Genocide," July 13, 2010. www.hrw.org.

Payton L. Knopf, "Rethinking Peacemaking in Darfur," Council on Foreign Relations, April 2011. www.cfr.org.

Nicholas D. Kristof, "Darfur in 2013 Sounds Awfully Familiar," *New York Times*, July 20, 2013. www.nytimes.com.

Colum Lynch, "The Silence in Sudan," *Foreign Policy*, May 7, 2012. www.foreignpolicy.com.

Colum Lynch, "'They Just Stood Watching,'" *Foreign Policy*, April 7, 2014. http://foreignpolicy.com.

Mahmood Mamdani, "The Politics of Naming: Genocide, Civil War, Insurgency," *London Review of Books*, March 8, 2007, vol. 29, no. 5, pp. 5–8.

Ben Mathis-Lilley, "Whistleblower Accuses UN of Lying, Covering Up Ongoing War in Darfur," *Slate*, April 9, 2014. www.slate.com.

Esther Pan, "Africa: The Darfur Crisis," Council on Foreign Relations, September 20, 2004. www.cfr.org.

Charles V. Pena and Christopher Prebie, "Despite Darfur's Horror, the US Should Just Stay Out," *Daily Star*, September 28, 2004. www.dailystar.com.

Samantha Power, "Dying in Darfur," *New Yorker*, August 30, 2004. www.newyorker.com.

John Prendergast, "The Answer to Darfur: How to Resolve the World's Hottest War," Center for American Progress, March 27, 2007. www.americanprogress.org.

Eric Reeves, "Darfur Is Getting Worse," *New Republic*, June 4, 2011. www.newrepublic.com.

Shmuel Rosner, "The Lessons of Darfur," *Slate*, January 9, 2008. www.slate.com.

Alex Whiting, "Darfur Risks Losing Another Generation to War—UNICEF," Thomas Reuters Foundation, May 8, 2014. www.trust.org.

G. Pascal Zachary, "A Problem from Hell," *Salon*, January 19, 2006. www.salon.com.

Websites

Eyes on Darfur (www.eyesondarfur.org). This project of Amnesty International provides evidence of atrocities in Darfur using commercially available high-definition satellite images of the region. It aims to enable action by private citizens, policy makers, and international courts to protect vulnerable villages in Sudan.

Survivors' Stories from Darfur (www.redcross.org.uk/What-we-do/Emergency-response/Past-emergency-appeals/Darfur-Crisis-Appeal-2007/Survivors-stories). A special section of the British Red Cross's website provides a number of personal stories of Darfur survivors and highlights the Red Cross's work in the region.

Film

Darfur Now (directed by Ted Braun, Warner Independent Pictures, 2007). This documentary examines the genocide in Darfur and the work of six individuals to bring public attention to the humanitarian crisis. The film includes the efforts of a student activist, a Darfurian rebel, the International Criminal Court prosecutor, a United Nations worker, a Hollywood actor and activist, and a community leader from a refugee camp.

Index